Prayer &
Multiple Intelligences

Who I Am Is How I Pray

Bernadette Stankard

PRAYER & Multiple Intelligences

WHO I AM IS HOW I PRAY

TWENTY THIRD 23rd
PUBLICATIONS

Dedication

To Ed, Nathaniel, and Petra who have taught
and continue to teach me so much about God.

Twenty-Third Publications
A Division of Bayard
185 Willow Street
P.O. Box 180
Mystic, CT 06355
(860) 536-2611 or (800) 321-0411
www.twentythirdpublications.com
ISBN:1-58595-512-4

Library of Congress Catalog Card Number: 2005923886
Printed in the U.S.A.

Contents

Introduction

The fullness of God is to behold God in everything.

Julian of Norwich, mystic

The need to reach and be one with God has been humanity's quest from the beginning of time. There is evidence that many caves adorned with paintings were actually places of worship. The paintings speak of rituals and sacred leaders, the early holy people who helped others on their journey to God.

Throughout the ages, people have chosen many paths in their search for a deeper relationship with God: the spoken word, meditation, spiritual works, music, art, dance, and communing with nature. The approaches to prayer have been as many and varied as the people who undertake a spiritual journey.

The one constant thread through these varied approaches, however, has been that each springs from one of the many different intelligences that people possess and through which they learn and communicate best. That's what this book is about: how multiple intelligences bring us into a deeper friendship with God, a friendship that fully awakens us to all that God intended us to be when we were first created.

Multiple intelligences is a theory that says each person has several intelligences: verbal-linguistic, logical-mathematical, musical-rhythmic, visual-spatial, bodily-kinesthetic, naturalistic, existential, interpersonal, and intrapersonal. Although people learn best through their strongest intelligence, they have the capability of developing all of them. Multiple intelligences, when applied to prayer, enable us to be fully awake—as God intended.

Note: In the Appendix to this book you will find a brief description of key characteristics of each intelligence, along with a few prayer ideas for each intelligence.

1

Relationship & Prayer

"I call you friends," Jesus once told his closest followers,
"because I have revealed myself entirely to you." Does that
sound like something that could happen in a mere moment?

Bill Huebsch

About ten o'clock one evening I was walking past my son's room and I heard laughter. Since he had gone to bed at least an hour earlier, and the bedside light was out indicating that his bedtime reading was done, I was surprised by the sound. As I peered into his room I saw that his eyes were closed and a smile played on his lips.

"Nathaniel," I called out tentatively. "Are you all right?" His eyes flew open.

"Sure, Mom, why?"

"I just heard someone laughing. Maybe you were dreaming."

"Oh, that. I wasn't dreaming. I was saying my prayers. I told a joke to God, and then God told me an even better one!"

This is prayer at its finest, sharing an intimately joyful relationship with the Creator. All too often when we talk of prayer, we become stuck on what we "must" do in order to pray well. We worry about our posture, or whether we are saying the right words, or if we are taking sufficient time to be in contact with God. We fret about the dry periods of our prayer life, and wonder if we have the right attitude when we approach this spiritual discipline.

Yet prayer is a relationship with God that can exist even if we are not aware of it.

I recall praying with each of our two children when they were babies. I would usually pray with them while sitting in the rocker. As I sat and nursed or comforted them, I admired and marveled at the beauty of their creation. I tickled their feet and laughed out loud at their funny faces. I sang songs that spoke of God. The rocker was the place where God touched my children and touched me, holding us, soothing us, revealing his care for us. Prayer was happening without me realizing it.

Tolbert McCarroll, an experienced religious educator, says, "The perfect model of a first prayer for a very young child is the essential tool for parenting—the rocking chair. As you rest in the peace of God, simply pick up your child and share your stillness." In such an atmosphere, not only our children but we ourselves meet the quiet of God and experience God as friend.

Growing the Relationship

Prayer is a relationship, and relationships grow gradually and in many different ways. If I talked with my husband only about how the house was operating, what the children did that day, or what the weather was like, our relationship would be shallow and somewhat lifeless. Instead, we take the time to talk, walk, dance, sing, laugh, and cry together. We take time for our relationship, and that time together takes many different forms. Our prayer relationship with God should be just as varied and rich.

That's where multiple intelligences come in. Although we learn through our strongest intelligence, we can also grow through working with the other intelligences. Applying this to prayer, we can pray most easily through our strongest intelligence, but we can also challenge ourselves to grow in our relationship with God through the other intelligences.

If we are to make prayer a way of life, we must make changes in our lives to ensure that this can happen. We are called to take the common and simple occurrences of everyday life and raise them to new heights of possibility and meaning, just as Jesus did. Witness the woman in adultery, who was raised up and forgiven by a savior who drew in the sand. This same savior used dirt and spit to bring about miraculous healings; with leftovers he fed a field full of his followers.

These same miraculous events happen today. Early on, one of the first phrases my children learned was "come and see." Whenever a new discovery was made, whenever something happened, the words, "come and see" invited, cajoled, and kept me running time and again throughout the day. Sometimes it meant they had discovered a bug or a flower; other times that they had fallen from a bike or found a newly-loosened tooth. All of these were moments of God for me and them.

The phrase "come and see" invites us to transform our lives. It helps us to make prayer a way of life, not just something set aside within our day. "Come and see" is the invitation our Lord gave to the new apostles. "Come and see" is the same invitation he extends to us today to discover, in each and every moment of our lives, the God who loves us so very much.

Hearing the Call

Now I invite you to "come and see." Find out what learning to pray with multiple intelligences can do for your relationship with God. God is not in a particular place or a particular time. God is surrounding us "as tightly as the clothes around our bodies," as Julian of Norwich, a sixteenth century mystic, once said. If this is true, there is no moment away from God; every moment is prayer. Every moment is sacred. Using our multiple intelligences will enable us to become childlike and see those sacred moments with more regularity.

God said to Julian of Norwich, "Because I love you, enjoy me. That would please me most." Come and see; maybe God wants to share a joke with you too.

2

My Journey with God

*Prayer is a relationship of person to person with all the
risk, the mystery, the dread, the confidence, the delight,
and the torment that lie in such a relationship."*

Jacques Maritain

My father had his first heart attack when I was only seven years
old. I remember it as a terrifying event. He was unable to
breathe and very obviously in pain. When emergency person-
nel gathered, I was pushed off to the side and told to not get in
the way. I didn't know what was happening except that my
world was falling apart. And that was the first time I remember
praying.

For many of us, prayer occurs most often when the needs of
life overwhelm us. We see God as one who dispenses help, one
who makes things better. That's how my seven-year-old mind
saw God when my father was in distress. God wasn't a part of
my life unless I was in trouble, unless I needed something.
Friendship with God was not part of my prayer experience.

Fortunately I didn't stay seven years old. As I grew up I came to know prayer more as a word to describe the time I spent with someone I loved. But it took me a while to arrive at that truth. During the journey I found out a lot about prayer and what it would ultimately mean to me.

My mother prayed regularly. I would often come upon her in a dark room, sitting in her chair, praying the rosary. Or I would find her sitting on the couch reading from her prayer books. When I asked her about what she was doing, she told me she was praying.

In my observation of her, I concluded that in order to pray you had to have the right books. I bought into that idea so fully that one day I went off to third grade with a purse full of prayer books. Whenever anyone asked me about them, I said with confidence that I used them to pray. After all, my mind reasoned, I did open them. I did read a word or two, and wasn't that what prayer was about? But this attempt at spirituality didn't last long because I found the books too heavy to lug around, and I always felt empty even after reading long prayers. I just wasn't connected.

My aunt, a nun, assured me that the Divine Office was the way to pray. She showed me her brown leather-bound missal and talked about how the sisters would pray in unison at different times of the day, chanting back and forth. I thought this approach sounded good, and so I recruited a girlfriend who I dragged into church each day at noon to "pray" the Office with me. Still something was missing.

My father reminisced about how, when he was growing up, the Angelus was said three times each day, at 6:00 AM, noon, and 6:00 PM. Vividly he described how he and his classmates would drop down to their knees to recite this ancient form of prayer to Mary. When I tried to use this approach, I often found myself in awkward or inappropriate places when it was time to say the Angelus. I still didn't feel connected.

During Forty Hours at our parish, the pastor emphasized that this special devotion was a time to meditate on the goodness of God, and how important it was to be quiet and listen. So I gazed at the monstrance, concentrating hard, straining my ears to hear God speak. I came away with only blurred vision.

My prayer life was going nowhere fast because I was looking in the wrong places. I liken this experience to the first years of my marriage. I had read lots of magazines and books and I thought I knew what romance was. It meant that because my husband, Ed, cared about me deeply, he would bring me flowers and candy and want to spend as much time as possible with me. And so I became upset when he didn't bring me flowers on Valentine's Day, but instead spent time fixing a leaky faucet and building a shelf for my books. I was so caught up in the "right" way to be romantic, to show love, that I forgot to open my eyes to the love that was right there, around me. I needed to see all the little things Ed was doing to show his love and care for me.

As a child growing up, I was doing that same thing with God. I was caught up in finding the "right" way to pray. What was the magic formula that would place me at the feet of God? What did I need to do to get God's attention?

During my freshman year in high school I happened upon a book called *Diary of a Country Priest*, by George Bernanos. It was a novel about the day-to-day life of a priest in France. Although I can't remember much about the book today, one line stays with me, a line that began to move me away from the trappings of prayer and more toward the essence. "The wish to pray is a prayer in itself," wrote Bernanos. I realized then that the times I struggled with wanting to pray but feeling that I wasn't doing it right were actually times of prayer. My wishing, my wanting, my trying to pray was itself prayer. As I wrestled with that concept I began to feel that maybe, just maybe, I was on the right track.

In God's Image

Not long after discovering the quote from Bernanos, I was asked by Fr. Clark, the pastor of our parish in Cleveland, Ohio, if I would visit some of the elderly people in the parish. I agreed to go, and he handed me the name and address of a woman, saying, "Just go and visit for a little while. She mostly wants someone to talk with."

The woman lived in a rundown apartment building on Superior Avenue, up a flight of steps. She was eighty-five years old, and her teeth were yellowed and broken, her hair matted and misshapen. The smell of cooking cabbage filled the air as I entered her apartment. I told her who I was, saying Fr. Clark had asked me to visit and find out if she wanted or needed anything.

"Come on in. Have a seat. Want some cabbage?"

I declined, not because I wasn't hungry, but rather because I was afraid of what might be in the cabbage. I stifled a gag reflex.

"How are you?" I managed to say, stumbling over the words.

With that question, the woman took over. She told me about her aches and pains, how much the neighborhood had changed, how she didn't like young people today, that the neighborhood was much nicer in the old days, that the church didn't care, that Fr. Clark was a nice man, that the politicians were all crooks, and that things would have been different if her son had lived.

"What happened to your son?" I asked, checking my watch.

Her eyes misted over as she slowly told me the story. Her son had been killed in World War II. She pulled out pictures, and I heard about his first bike ride and his first day at school, about the day he left for war and the day the telegram arrived. Realizing that the sky outside had darkened and feeling uncomfortable with her grief, I told the woman that I had to leave. Gruffly, she nodded goodbye and closed the door. I found myself in the hall, feeling as if the conversation hadn't taken place.

When I reached the sidewalk, I saw a small boy playing marbles with a friend in front of the apartment building next door. Briefly he looked up at me as I passed by. I didn't know what was happening at that moment, but today I can look back and know God spoke to me in that moment. The boy's eyes were wide and twinkling as a smile crossed his face. I smiled back, and as I did the story of the young man going off to war came back to me. The young man was someone who had played and cried and laughed and loved his mother. He was a child of God, and his mother was a child of God. God was present in each of them, and God was present in the boys playing marbles on the sidewalk in front of me. Indeed, God was present in me.

The thought that God is with us at all times, in all places, in all circumstances was overwhelming to me. Why was I always trying to find God when God is right here with me? That day was a turning point for me. I realized that God is present all the time, not just in church or just during special prayer times. God is always with me, which meant I could talk with God any time, in any place. When I encountered the boy playing marbles on the street, some of the pieces of my prayer puzzle began to fall into place.

A few days later, in religion class, we were giving our reports on saints. Each of us had researched a saint and prepared a presentation for the class. Christine Josephitis had chosen St. Teresa of Avila. As she read her report, my mind started to wander—after all, it was the fifth presentation of the day. The sun was streaming through the windows and I felt my eyes grow heavy. Suddenly they shot open; Christine was quoting St. Teresa:

> Christ has no body now on earth but yours. You are the only hands with which he can do his work. Yours are the only feet with which he can go about the world. Yours are the only eyes through which his compassion can shine forth upon a troubled world. Christ has no body on earth now but yours.

Memories of the past struggle flooded back. I would be Jesus to others through my own uniqueness. I would talk with God through my own personality. I would listen to God with everything that made up my life. I would be in a friendship with God that was different from all others.

On that day, I was still a long way from a real understanding of prayer, but it was a beginning. The concept of prayer as relationship was growing slowly but surely, by the grace of God.

Praying with Your Whole Person

During my senior year in high school, a Carmelite priest came to our parish for a mission. Since I worked at the rectory each day after school answering the phones and recording the Sunday envelopes, I saw him more than just at the mission services. Whenever I ran into this priest, he was always whistling or singing. One day I worked up enough courage to ask him if he always did that.

"Of course I do. It's one of the ways I keep in touch with God."

My eyebrows rose. "Whistling keeps you in touch with God?"

He nodded. "I always liked to whistle or sing when I was growing up. Sometimes it was a sad melody, sometimes happy, sometimes a melody with no rhyme or reason. But the important thing was that it made me feel better. Whistling made me work out whatever it was that was making me sad, or it made me intensify whatever it was that was making me happy."

"Yes, but how does that keep you in touch with God?"

"Well, one day when I was praying, reciting the Divine Office, I felt like whistling." He looked at me and smiled. "Of course, you couldn't very well do that in a church with a group of monks around you. But later that day, I realized that my urge to whistle was really a response to God. My heart was so grateful for the things God had done for me at that point in my life, I just wanted to whistle a tune of thanks. I couldn't identify the song; I knew only that I wanted to whistle—like the feeling you get sometimes when you want to shout because there is almost too much inside and you have to make room."

I could relate to that. Lots of times, having seven sisters and brothers, I wanted to shout to be heard.

"So you took to whistling to thank God?" I was still skeptical.

"Sort of. It wasn't just to give thanks, though. It was also to let off steam, to cry, whatever. Whistling, humming, singing— they all give me a way to talk to God that is very much a part of me."

"But that's not being reverent," I blurted out.

The priest smiled again. "Whenever you are yourself and aware of God with you, that's what makes up reverence. God wants to see and hold and talk with me as me, not as someone I would hope to be or as someone I am told to be."

He was talking about prayer with added personality—not only being yourself in prayer but using your body and soul in order to do so. And if that meant whistling, then if you wanted an honest relationship, you had to whistle.

Yet another door to understanding my own way of prayer opened when I was a freshman in college. I had journeyed down to Mississippi to work at a Pax Christi house in Greenwood. It was 1967 and tensions were high on the civil rights front. Our assignment was simple: to teach religion, talk with the people who lived there, register people to vote, tutor—in short, do whatever needed to be done.

One day, during our evening prayer time, we were joined by an African-American woman from the community. The mother of seven children, she felt passionately that all her children should have the opportunity to educate themselves and be whatever they wanted to be. She would often say, "God loves my children as much as the white children."

It had been a particularly tiring and frustrating day, and we were all questioning our commitment to change the world. Someone in the group started to sing, "We Shall Not Be Moved." Slowly each of us joined in. The woman joined in too, her eyes closed, her mind seeming to consider the words carefully. Suddenly, she stood up, her body moving slowly and fluidly, her hands clenching and then releasing, following whatever she had let go into the air as if it were being carried up to God by angels. As she moved with grace and beauty throughout the church, my eyes and heart took it all in. Here before me was prayer. This woman was using her body and her spirit to pour out her frustrations before God, her friend.

St. Thérèse of Lisieux said, "With me, prayer is a lifting up of the heart, a look towards heaven, a cry of gratitude and love uttered equally in sorrow and joy; in a word, something noble, supernatural, which enlarges my soul and unites it to God." That day, the woman had done just that with the wondrous gift God gave her: her body.

We too have that gift but too often when we pray we forget we are soul *and* body. This woman revealed that the body is an integral part of prayer, enabling us to say things we cannot put into words.

Part of a Bigger Family

When I returned to school from Mississippi, I had the opportunity to attend a Cursillo, a retreat format that was quite popular in the 1970s. It was a good time for introspection, but perhaps even more so, it was time for me to learn the importance of praying with and for others.

During a Cursillo, the retreatants—called Cursillistas (female) or Cursillistos (male)—receive letters from friends, family, and coworkers, telling them that people have been praying for them throughout the entire weekend. As I opened and read my letters, I was reminded of my senior year in high school when I was hospitalized for an appendectomy. I was there for a week following the operation, and every day my best friend, Vida Habjan, would come to visit. She would tell me about what went on in class that day, what was happening to whom, and who had asked about me. She encouraged me to hurry up and get better.

The letters I received at the Cursillo brought back this memory and showed me what a great gift Vida had been. She cared enough to take the time to remember me and think of me as she went through her day. She made sure I wasn't forgotten, and she reminded me I was a part of a larger family.

Those Cursillo letters told me something: we are all part of the same family. God is a Friend to each of us. Together we can approach God and grow not only in our relationship with God, but also in our relationship with each other. The significant piece of the puzzle fell into place that day. I realized that prayer is all about relationship with God as well as with the world God created.

Putting It All Together

Growing up, my stumbling block to prayer was that I was trying to pray in parts. I thought my relationship with God would be formed by what I did or did not do. If I set time aside for God, a relationship would take place. If I said the right words, God would answer. If I assumed the right position, God would notice me. But what I really needed to see was that all these parts were merely pieces of the whole of prayer.

Yet in parts, God showed me the mystery of the whole. All the little incidents, all the insights over the years, led to one important truth: prayer is being in total relationship with God. This relationship with God is about being me and coming to God with my whole being—with words, with song, with movement, with nature, with the world, and with others.

Years after this discovery, as I began to work with multiple intelligences in the classroom, I was happy to find their use could also help me nurture this total relationship with my Creator. Applying the theory to my prayer life, I found I was better able to pray with my whole person, to stretch myself and find myself as a wondrous creature of God. No longer could I segment my time with God. I was called to a relationship with God which included both being me and expressing myself with all my foibles and gifts.

I don't claim to be an expert on prayer; all I can share is my experience with God. Picasso once said, "Painting cannot be taught." This is true of prayer as well. No one can teach you to pray, but we can journey together and learn from each other. We take from one another what helps us draw closer to God.

On the following pages, I offer some of the insights I continue to gain on my spiritual journey. When I pray using the multiple intelligences, amazing things happen. I come to understand more fully the words written in Psalm 34: "Taste and see that the Lord is good." For God is indeed tasty goodness.

3

Everyone Has Different Intelligences

If you want to teach something that is important,
there is more than one way to teach it.

Howard Gardner, Harvard University Professor

The theory of multiple intelligences is nothing new. In 1983, Howard Gardner, professor of education at Harvard University, published *Frames of Mind: The Theory of Multiple Intelligences*. In it he introduced the idea that the traditional notion of intelligence based on IQ testing is very limited.

In the past, intelligence was determined by one of two tests: The Stanford-Binet and the Wechsler Intelligence Scale for Children. Testing intelligence began around 1905 in Paris when the French government asked two psychologists, Alfred Binet and Theodore Simon, to develop a test that would determine which students would do well and which would fail in the school system. Revised in the 1930s by Lewis Terman at Stanford University, the test was renamed the Stanford-Binet, and intelligence was given a quotient—the ratio of mental age to chronological age. Around this same time, psychologist David Wechsler was developing intelligence tests for both children and adults. Both of these tests are still used regularly today.

Both of these assessment tools, however, rely heavily on verbal and mathematical skills. Often the gifts of children and adults who do not have strengths in these areas are overlooked. In addition, many school systems are heavily geared toward verbal-linguistic and logical-mathematical intelligences, leaving children and adults who are weaker in these areas frustrated or continually facing failure.

With the publication of Gardner's book, the situation slowly began to change. Gardner urged school systems to re-design themselves in order to be responsive to individual cognitive differences. Telling teachers to "know as much as you can about the kids rather than make them pass through the same eye of the needle," Gardner put forth the theory of multiple intelligences so all children and adults would have the opportunity to reach their highest potential.

Gardner's theory comes from extensive research done on the brain. His work included interviews, tests, and research on hundreds of individuals. His study addressed stroke and accident victims, prodigies, autistic individuals, those with learning disabilities, idiot savants, and people from many cultures.

What came out of all this work was the conclusion that there is not one fixed, inborn trait that dominates all the skills, problem-solving strategies, and learning abilities people possess. Instead, intelligence is centered in many different areas of the brain. All these areas are interconnected, work independently and yet rely on each other, and, most importantly, can be developed under the right conditions.

Gardner theorized that there are many intelligences. Each person learns through his or her strongest intelligence and has the capacity to develop other intelligences during a lifetime. Needless to say, this theory shook up the educational system, which was used to being able to "test" and "measure" intelligence in order to determine who was smart and who wasn't. Instead, if they bought into Gardner's theory, they needed to look at individuals, each having different ways to learn and the potential for strengthening other intelligences.

Gardner recognized numerous intelligences, of which nine have been identified.

Verbal-linguistic intelligence is a sensitivity to the sounds, meanings, order, and rhythm of words. Individuals having strength in this area love to play with words, have highly developed auditory skills, and usually have a good memory for people and places. People strong in this intelligence love to read, write, and tell stories, and include writers, public speakers, comedians, poets and actors.

Pope John Paul II was strong in this intelligence. A man fluent in many languages, John Paul had many books to his credit. His facility with words astounded people during his papacy. Shakespeare, Maya Angelou, and J.K. Rowling also exhibit this intelligence. Good lawyers are certainly blessed with it. Verbal-linguistic intelligence is emphasized in school systems across our country.

Logical-mathematical intelligence is the capacity and sensitivity to spot logical or numerical patterns. It is the ability to handle long chains of reasoning. This intelligence of scientific thinking enables people to explore and see the progression of events through a given time period. It sees the relationship of one thing to another. Our scientists, philosophers, and mathematicians are strong in this intelligence. The scientist Galileo exhibited this intelligence as he explored the universe and its many mysteries. This is the intelligence through which science shows us the existence of God.

Musical-rhythmic intelligence is the ability to produce and appreciate rhythm, pitch, timbre, and various forms of musical expression. Someone strong in this intelligence is sensitive to the sounds of the environment and the human voice as well as to musical instruments. All the great classical composers like Mozart, Bach, Beethoven, and Debussy made great use of this intelligence. Today we see it manifest in composers like John Williams, Stephen Sondheim, and Andrew Lloyd Webber.

Visual-spatial intelligence, or the intelligence of pictures and images, enables one to perceive the visual world accurately, and then recreate his or her experience through form, color, shape, and texture. Individuals with strength in this area envision something in the mind's eye and are able to transfer it to a concrete representation. This is the intelligence of architects, sculptors, and engineers. Walking into the house known as Fallingwater, in Pennsylvania, you can almost feel Frank Lloyd Wright taking the image of a waterfall and putting dimension to it. Leonardo Da Vinci filled notebook upon notebook with sketches and worked to put shape to them. Michelangelo saw David in the slab of marble even before others began to see the emerging form.

Bodily-kinesthetic intelligence is the ability to use the body to express emotion, as in dance, body language, and sports. It is the ability to learn by doing and involves the whole body. Surgeons, dancers, craftsmen, and athletes are strong in this intelligence. We see this intelligence everyday on television. It can be seen in sitcoms and dramas, during basketball and football games and on PBS specials that highlight the great ballet dancers of our time. We watch with awe as talented magicians like Harry Houdini use their bodies to mesmerize us with their magic. Some of us use this intelligence in dance classes, softball games, and other activities that involve the body.

Naturalist intelligence is manifest in those who are very sensitive to all features of the natural world. There is a strong ability among individuals with this intelligence to recognize and categorize plants, animals, and other objects in nature. They have the capacity to see nature operating on a larger scale. Farmers, horticulturists, and zoologists exhibit strength in this intelligence. We celebrate this intelligence in Sacajawea who accompanied Lewis and Clark on their trek west. She was able to guide them well because of her sensitivity to the world around her. Jane Goodall, using her naturalist intelligence, opened up the world of primates to us, filling us with wonder about the complex communities of these creatures.

Intrapersonal intelligence is the knowledge of the internal aspects of self in areas such as feelings, emotional responses, self-reflection and an intuitive sense about spiritual realities. Individuals with strength in this intelligence are good at focusing, concentrating, and thinking things through. They have a strong sense of self, are confident, and enjoy working alone. They know their strengths and abilities. They are discoverers and leaders.

Charles Lindbergh needed his intrapersonal intelligence to make his landmark flight to Paris in 1927. He had to rely on himself and his abilities to accomplish the task of flying solo across the Atlantic.

Interpersonal intelligence is the ability to detect and respond appropriately to the moods, motivations, and desires of others. People strong in this intelligence have the ability to work cooperatively in a group as well as to communicate both verbally and non-verbally with other people. Teachers, clinicians, salespeople, politicians, and preachers are strong in this intelligence.

Dr. Martin Luther King, Jr., had strong interpersonal intelligence. He reached people, empathized with them, and challenged them to move beyond their present state. With this intelligence, Mohandas Gandhi drew thousands of people into his nonviolent protests against the British Empire. Every day Oprah Winfrey uses her interpersonal intelligence to reach millions of people on a variety of topics.

Existential intelligence is the sensitivity and capacity to tackle profound questions of human existence, such as what is the meaning of life, why do we die, and how did we get here. People strong in this intelligence are the Aristotles, the Einsteins, the Platos of the world.

Because he asked profound questions, Albert Einstein worked his entire life for international peace. Even his last letter to Bertrand Russell pleaded for peace. Confucius, another great thinker who was strong in existential intelligence, worked to bring an understanding of life to the common people, always urging them to consider deep questions.

Igniting Our Passions

All these intelligences, when nurtured, give people plenty of enrichment opportunities for discovering their passions. Gardner cites Yehudi Menuhin, a musical genius who, at three, was enchanted with the sound of the violin. He insisted on having his own instrument; his parents agreed, and that stimulation of his musical intelligence led to a lifetime of great musical passion. Gardner argues that we must offer people the chance to encounter such "crystallizing experiences"—events that shape the future—so that individuals become excited about learning and about the world around them.

So what does all this have to do with prayer? I refer you to Hildegard of Bingen, one of the great mystics of the Church, who said, "Be not lax in celebrating. Be not lazy in the festive service of God. Be ablaze with enthusiasm. Let us be an alive burning offering before the altar of God." How often do we see this advice at work in our prayer, either individually or as a community? Too often we make our prayer dull and duty-driven. We lose the joy that is part of any good love relationship.

A few years ago while on vacation, I went to a church in Ohio. I was looking forward to a good celebration of liturgy, but unfortunately, it was not to be. The music, while contemporary, was sung like a funeral dirge, slow and ponderous. The priest mumbled through most of the Mass and when he came to the words of consecration, it sounded as if he were totally bored with God. At the sign of peace, the people around me offered a limp handshake or nothing at all. At the close of the Mass, following the words, "Go in peace to love and serve the Lord," the response was barely audible.

I left the church depressed. These were people who had heard the good news, who had been chosen by Jesus to spread the gospel—yet there was no indication that God was alive in them. This community was not ablaze in its worship. Hildegard would have been disappointed.

In the play *Fiddler on the Roof,* Teyve sings a song to life. The words pour forth with passion and great appreciation for the gift he has in being alive in that moment with his friends, his family, and his God. We too should sing as Teyve did. God has given us amazing gifts: our lives, the world around us, the friends and family who love us. God has gifted us with a body that does things a computer can only begin to duplicate, a soul that can appreciate fine art and the beginning scribbles of a toddler, a mind that can make a grocery list and understand the great philosophers of the world.

When we allow ourselves to experiment with the different intelligences and to identify that intelligence which is strongest for us, through which we learn best, we open the door to allow enthusiasm—from the Greek word *entheo,* which translates to "God within"—to grow in our faith.

One of the best qualities of a good relationship is that the faces of each still light up when one sees the other. There is an excitement about the fact that they are together again, that they have a chance to grow closer. How many times do you see this quality when people are talking about their relationship with God?

My relationship with God is so important to me, so exciting that I *want* to talk about it. I *want* to sing about it. I *want* to dance. I *want* to be silent in God's presence. This is a God who loved me enough to create me, who sustained me through a personal crisis, who has blessed me with a wonderful family, who died for me, who has given me a world replete with wonder, and who has cared for me like a child. This God is exciting. This God is magical. This God deserves enthusiasm from us.

Using multiple intelligences in prayer can help us rekindle enthusiasm or begin to develop it. Multiple intelligences can allow us to discover how best to pray and then expand our prayer in new ways.

Awakening the Sleeping Dragon

In his book *Winter Dreams and Other Such Friendly Dragons,* Joseph Junknialis tells the story of Crisst, a dragon who was ferocious, mean-spirited, and breathed forth fiery hate. He thought nothing of smashing villages and destroying crops, until one day he met a knight named John.

John wore no armor and carried no sword. This confused Crisst. During that moment of confusion, John raced under the dragon's belly and grabbed his tail. Anyone who knows anything about dragons knows that the tail is their one vulnerable spot. Crisst thought he was done for. He waited for John to pick up Crisst's own sword and drive it through his heart. But instead the knight ignored the sword and started to walk away. Crisst shouted after him, asking why the knight didn't kill him. John turned to him and said, "I will not slay you for tonight is Christmas, one of the most peaceful nights of the year." And with that he walked away.

Crisst was so moved by the act of kindness that he no longer went about the countryside doing evil. Instead he helped in whatever way he could. The story, however, doesn't end there. Every year around Christmas, Crisst, in honor of John's kindness, would go throughout the land inviting his fellow dragons to a party with the finest of food and drink and camaraderie. It became quite the event, one that none of the dragons wanted to miss.

Crisst did this every year with enthusiasm and care, not only to mark the tremendous act of kindness—the new life given to him by John—but also to make sure that there were no dragons to invade people's lives during the season of Christmas.

We are like Crisst. We have been redeemed by a God who cared enough to touch us with love, a God who promised us eternal life. We need to travel the countryside and let people know this good news.

Using multiple intelligences in your prayer life will awaken the sleeping dragon. Let's see how.

4

Praying All Ways with the Intelligences

God pops up everywhere, all the time in my life.
I find myself saying "Ah, there's God again."

Edwina Gately

One of my most delightful times teaching religious education was when I had a preschool class. The class included three-, four-, and five-year-olds. The classroom used a Montessori approach, which meant that after a short time together for the lesson, the children were free to roam around the room and work in different areas which furthered the theme. As a facilitator and observer, I moved around the room, answering questions, asking questions, and listening. During this time of listening, I was privileged to hear some pretty amazing things about God.

During a lesson on baptism, a five-year-old commented on the strength of God. "God's very strong because God can clean up anything. Sort of like Mr. Clean. Only God does sins and those are harder to clean. But it's easy for God." During a lesson on creation, a little girl talked about rainbows and how everything God made was full of color. "God did it so we wouldn't be bored, so we would always have something new to look at." A session on prayer yielded this from a little four-year-old, "God made the world magic." When I commented on how nice that was, she added, "Yep, God made it magic. It's up to us to find the surprises."

It *is* up to us to find the surprises God offers. In our relationship with God, it is up to us to be open to everything that relationship entails. We are not called to close doors; we are called to open them and then to walk through them.

One of the doors to open is the one marked "multiple intelligences." And then we need to walk through and experience everything it has to offer. When you pray with your strongest intelligence and open yourself to developing the other intelligences, you allow God to work in your life with all God's fullness. You, like Edwina Gately, will see God "pop up" all over.

God reaches out and touches us throughout the day. Spreading a bit of peanut butter on a piece of bread? God is like peanut butter, a staple in our life, sticking with us throughout everything. Washing windows? Much like Windex, the grace of God enables us to wipe away the sins in our lives. The more we become aware of God around us, the more we look on prayer as a relationship, and the more we use multiple intelligences to reach out to God. We are in prayer with God throughout the day.

Using multiple intelligences in prayer is not new. People have been doing it throughout history. Whenever someone has danced before God, whenever anyone has shouted out to God in anger or frustration, whenever someone has composed a poem of praise—each has been using multiple intelligences. Multiple intelligences are the capabilities given by God to each and everyone of us. Although there is one particular intelligence through which we best learn, and through which we best pray, the other intelligences are still there to help us pray with our whole person, to help us open those doors that will show us new and different aspects of God.

A prayer from New Guinea reads, "Lord, oil the hinges of our hearts' doors that they may swing gently and easily to welcome your coming." The writer of this prayer had the right idea. Keep the door open and become aware of the many times and many ways when God comes into our lives.

Opening the Door

It was the week before Christmas, and my husband, Ed, and I were in a small town called Marfa in southwest Texas working as family ministers at St. Mary's Parish. It was a town of barely two thousand, in the middle of nowhere with the Chianti Mountains as a backdrop and endless ranches dotting the landscape.

We were just coming to terms with spending Christmas in Marfa without any family. A two-thousand-mile trip back home in our old Volkswagen bug was not possible. We had been married for just over three years and each Christmas together we had journeyed back to visit Ed's mother in New York or to my parents' home in Cleveland. That was not to be this year.

We tried to make the best of it, but with little money to spend—we couldn't even afford a tree—and in a town that was barely beginning to accept us, we didn't hold much hope that this would be a Christmas to remember. How wrong we were!

One evening, I was working in the kitchen, cleaning up after a church meeting we had had in our house. Ed was in our living room, putting up the folding chairs we had borrowed from the church and sweeping the dust off the floor. We had decided we would head to bed early and talk about how the two of us would spend Christmas. As I put the last dish up in the cupboard, I heard a knock at the side door. I went over to answer it and was surprised to see several of the teens from the church choir.

"Hi guys," I said. "What are you up to?"

Lionel, the president of the choir, just winked at me and turned to talk to the others behind him. "Be careful not to break any branches." And with that caution, the group surged forward through the door and into our living room with a tree.

I can't say it was much to look at, but it was indeed an evergreen tree, a tree which one of the boys was busy nailing to a stand. Becky, another choir member, asked "Can we take off this table cloth?" indicating the one spread on our dining room table. I nodded and then watched as they folded the cloth and began to spread construction paper, glue, glitter, tape and scissors out on the table. Becky answered my puzzled expression. "We're going to make ornaments for the tree."

The room was now filled with activity. Some of the kids were at the table making stars and candles and paper chains. Someone had put Christmas music on our stereo, and some were out in the kitchen mixing up cookies. The laughter and conversation continued until the tree was indeed covered with ornaments and our stomachs filled with cookies.

As Ed and I started to thank the group, Lionel stopped us and said, "We're not done yet." And with that Becky pulled out her last package: clay. Everyone was going to fashion a figure for our stable. You could hear the bulls in the backyard as the room quieted with the job of making the crèche. It wasn't a work of art but it was a work of love. As we each placed our figures in the stable under the newly decorated tree, I felt a surge of love for each of the kids and realized that God was present during the entire evening.

The kids had helped us experience God interpersonally. With the tree in place, I knew that my longing for the trappings of Christmas had become real through visual-spatial intelligence. As Lionel put on the music, the musical-rhythmic door opened. When George Williams told me what kind of fir the tree was, the naturalist intelligence came into play, and as we all worked on our ornaments and on the manger figures, the bodily-kinesthetic door opened. As I stood with Ed after the kids left and admired the tree by the light of the gas heater, I knew God was speaking to me through intrapersonal intelligence, telling me once again to open my mind and heart. All doors lead to God and just need to be opened.

That evening was truly an evening of prayer. From the moment I saw the teenagers outside with the tree, I knew that God was alive and magic was afoot.

No "Right Way" To Pray

Encounters like the one I have just described illustrate that there is no "right way" to pray. Using multiple intelligences in prayer opens me to see that there are many ways to pray. It helps me know that prayer is as individual as the person who is praying, and it can be expressed through art, dance, quiet contemplation, or other creative ways.

Because each of us is uniquely created, we each have to find our own right path to prayer. Multiple intelligences allow us to feel comfortable with different approaches. We don't have to feel guilty if we want to raise up our hands in prayer. We need not feel odd if we want to let the melody running through our heads come out in praise of God. We don't have to dismiss an encounter in which we shared a part of our lives with another because it did not seem prayer-like. All of these instances are prayer at its finest. All of them are ways to praise God and enter into a relationship with God. All of them are enhanced by becoming aware of and using multiple intelligences.

At the parish where my husband and I ministered in northern Minnesota, there was a woman named Marie who would sit at the end of the last pew in church every day. During Mass she would say the prayers very loudly, laugh at different parts of the homily, be the only one who would add names to the prayers of petition, and in general, be what some considered a nuisance and distraction. To further complicate things, Marie would greet each person as they left the church, smiling and shaking their hands.

Marie probably hadn't read any books on prayer. She didn't know any fancy approaches, but what she did know was that she had to pray as "Marie." She was a very interpersonal individual who communicated to the congregation that God cared about each and every one of them. Marie did this by sharing, in a very concrete, warm way, the presence of God she received through Mass.

There is no magic formula for prayer. Prayer using multiple intelligences means taking a leap beyond your comfort zone. It means being aware of prayer as a relationship and then thinking of all the ways you can nurture that relationship. All you have to do is begin. There is no right place, no right time except here and now to work on your relationship with God.

As you begin to use multiple intelligences in your prayer life, go slowly. Like a toddler learning to walk, take small steps as you hang onto the furniture of prayer until the magic moment when you let go and take that first step alone. Let go and let God operate your prayer life. Stop trying to control it and you will find that your prayer will naturally draw on the different intelligences. God is in the driver's seat and God wants all of us, not bits and pieces.

Using multiple intelligences in our prayer lives allows us to give our whole selves to God.

5

How to Begin

All real prayer must begin in wonder.

Tad Dunne, artist and writer

Growing up, I was taught that whenever a siren sounded, I should stop right away and say a prayer for the person, the family, and the police or firefighters involved in the emergency. This action quickly became second nature. I would wonder about the person and family I was praying for, what they might be going through. One time, when I heard the sirens while I was at school, I prayed, not realizing that I was praying for my father and my own family that day. My father had had a stroke but would soon recover, learning once again to walk and talk. Without even knowing who we were, the people who had prayed the same siren prayer helped my family that day.

The telephone rings. Immediately we wonder who is calling. If we have call-waiting, the mystery is taken away and we must only make the decision to answer or not to answer. How many times have we picked up that phone to hear the voice of someone in need or the proclamation of a glorious achievement?

Simple actions like these are something that can start each of us on the path of using multiple intelligences in prayer. Let the telephone and the siren not only remind you of God but of the person who is calling or in need. Being aware of these reminders is sometimes referred to as mindfulness or attentiveness, but in all their simplicity they are a call to prayer.

As we have seen, prayer is a relationship that encompasses our entire person, our entire life. It is a call to attend to all the aspects that will draw us into that relationship. Hearing the siren, listening to the ring of the phone, spreading peanut butter—all of these are visual-spatial reminders of that call.

Another simple call to prayer is the alarm clock. As the alarm sounds and you are drawn to consciousness, say, "This is the day the Lord has made. Let me be glad and rejoice."

The first time I tried this, I'm afraid God received my words in a not-too-pleasant tone of voice—one only slightly better than that of an angry cheetah who lost her prey. As the days went by, my tone softened. Then one day I realized the depth of what I was saying: this *is* the day the Lord has made, and I have been graciously given another day to enjoy, relish, and grow in. The encounter which started out as a surly acknowledgement of the day I always took for granted turned into a time of gratitude for having the day in the first place, and for the chance to use it for the glory of my Creator.

Taking Baby Steps

There are hundreds of ways to take baby steps toward giving your whole self in prayer. And these steps are as many and varied as our world. Be creative in your approach to your friendship with God. Think of day-to-day situations in which you can use various techniques as springboards to the divine.

Here are a few examples:

• Everyone has counted to ten to avoid an angry confrontation or a loss of temper. Next time try counting, "One for God, two for God…" and see the difference it makes.

• Use your computer screensaver to remind yourself of God during work. Perhaps it could display "Be glad and rejoice," or "Each person is a God-holder."

• If you don't currently pray before meals, start doing so.

• As you fill up your gas tank, take time to visualize yourself being filled up with God.

These are just a few of the hundreds of ways throughout the day you can take steps toward God.

Another step toward prayer using multiple intelligences is taking time each morning to create three pages in a stream of consciousness. This is where you write or draw or otherwise express yourself without consciously thinking about it, just simply putting down what comes into your mind at the moment. Julia Cameron, author of *The Artist's Way*, suggests this technique for those who wish to write or draw or be more creative. I started doing this exercise hoping to build my creativity and found instead that it became an encounter with God.

Early on I wrote what I considered stupid stuff:

The light pull is dangling and swinging and reminding me of jungle vines. It is hot and muggy out and I haven't even stepped out the door. All the plants seem droopy from the continuous heat we've had. I have to remember to take the books back to the library. Ah, the dog just walked into the living room. I can still hear Ed snoring. I'm not ready to get into everything. I wish I could have slept longer.

The stream of consciousness was all the "stuff" I needed to

get done or that I noticed only as a by product of how it affected me. As I persisted in writing these morning pages, something changed: God stepped in.

I'm feeling apprehensive about this trip to Manhattan. Will I be able to drive the van? Will I be accepted by the kids and not get witchy? God, I'm so wrapped up in fear. It is almost as if I cannot do anything on my own. I need help in chasing this fear away. *I can help you, Bernadette. You have to trust in me.* But I'm helpless, God. *You're not concentrating on the present moment. Not concentrating on the here and now. You really need to remember this. Just trust, Bernie.*

Throughout my entries, the pronouns changed according to who was talking. My pages became an exchange between God and me. I found that as I wrote my concerns God answered them, giving me direction and support, saying just the right thing and often something I didn't want to hear. The act of writing down my thoughts in a stream of consciousness caused me to open my mind to hearing God amid all the jumble of "stuff." God was looking beyond my thoughts and waiting, anxious to be in a relationship with me.

Journaling has long been encouraged as a way of readying yourself for prayer. Unlike writing in a stream of consciousness, journaling is often more directed, addressing a particular area in your life or a time in your life and dealing with questions such as, "What has touched me in this experience?" or "Why did I respond that way?" With stream of consciousness writing, you cannot be as structured. You have to allow whatever is in your mind at the time to freely come out, and from those thoughts, God can speak.

Lots of times God speaks in my stream-of-consciousness

pages and says things I don't want to hear or that seem to have no significance. It is only as I go about my day that I am able to see what God was trying to point out to me. The act of working from your stream of consciousness frees up your mind to surface thoughts, ideas, and challenges you should be addressing. Once we allow God room to come in, we can find those surprises I referred to earlier.

One last step you might consider is a form of guided meditation, which is a very simple way to open your heart to discover what's there. It also allows God to speak without our interference.

To begin, close your eyes and calm yourself. Become aware of God. When you are ready, tell God what's happening in your life, much as you would a good friend. Tell God everything, even your secrets because God is your best friend.

As you move along, talk with God about anyone who is uppermost in your mind, someone you would like to place before God. Take time together with God to love the people you have remembered. Love together the different things that make up these people.

Next, don't say anything. Just become quiet and listen, Feel God loving you. Dwell on this and when you are ready, express to God how this makes you feel.

This prayer time will allow you to enter the day, or move on to another activity, not only refreshed but ever more aware of God right with you.

During a session on prayer with a group of catechists in a small town in Kansas, I opened the gathering with this prayer, leading the group slowly through the steps. As the prayer drew to a natural close for each participant, we continued on with the session. This gathering proved to be one of the best sessions on prayer I have ever presented, one in which I felt a great unity with each participant. Without a doubt, I attribute its success to the time each of us spent developing a conscious awareness of God and listening to how much God loves us.

Now it's time to move on to prayer experiences that address a particular intelligence. As with most things in life, there is no prayer, no exercise that uses just one intelligence. The intelligences overlap, and rightfully so. This is our Creator urging us to go beyond what we are comfortable with, to challenge ourselves by going beyond the intelligence through which we learn best.

In the chapter for each intelligence, the prayer encounter will primarily address that intelligence. Remember, though, that the intelligences do overlap so that a prayer suggestion for one intelligence might easily be effective for another. I have noted some of those instances. You will also see that some appear to be exercises and not prayer. It is important to remember that as long as you have the correct mindset, as long as you are doing something with the intent of building your relationship with God, it is prayer.

6

Praying with Verbal-Linguistic Intelligence

Your Father in heaven knows what you need
before you ask him, so you should pray like this:
Our Father who are in heaven....

Matthew 6:8–9

The stage was set with a priedieu, a light from above shining on it: nothing more. Once the audience quieted, a solitary man came out and knelt. After rubbing his eyes and yawning, he began to pray fast and matter-of-factly.

"Our Father who...."

"Yes?" a voice boomed offstage.

The man looked around, puzzled by the "noise" he heard. Shrugging it off, he continued.

"Our Father who....."

"Yes, what is it?" the voice asked.

Again the man looked around, concern clouding his eyes.

"God?" his timid voice asked.

"Yes. You called me and I answered."

And so the prayer continued, with God interrupting to make sure the man really knew what he was saying, that the words were not just words but were to be spoken from the heart.

When we use our verbal-linguistic intelligence in prayer, we invite God to do with us what he did with the man saying the Our Father. God asks us to stop and think, listen, put power behind the words. We invite God to be an active part of the words we use and say. When we use verbal-linguistic intelligence in prayer, we can no longer just say the words. We find that the words are active and demand participation and a response. Verbal-linguistic intelligence will help our prayer be more than just words. It will instill a life to our words and deepen our encounter with God.

Verbal linguistic intelligence is the intelligence of words. People strong in this intelligence have a high sensitivity to the sounds, rhythms, and meanings of words, along with a sensitivity to the different functions of language. They have great auditory skills and enjoy reading and writing. This is a powerful intelligence that carries with it the capacity to paint strong word pictures.

When using this intelligence in prayer, look for good books to draw from. Use Scripture and the words of the great teachers of the church liberally, but don't close yourself off from using what some people term secular material. Often this material challenges people with strong verbal-linguistic intelligence to use their skills along with other intelligences, such as logical-mathematical, to make connections with God. Individuals with verbal-linguistic strength would do well to use poetry, humor, storytelling, and writing in their prayer.

Here are a few possibilities to start you on your verbal-linguistic prayer journey.

• Take a prayer you are very familiar with and say it in different ways. For instance, say the Our Father as if you are bored to tears. Listen to what is going on in your heart as you do this. Repeat it out loud in a tone of great enthusiasm. Again, listen. Often it is a good idea to take the emotion that is uppermost in your mind and say the prayer out loud with that emotion in your voice. Reflection will often bring insights into what you are experiencing and why.

• Record a story from Scripture, the news, or a book you are reading. You might consider telling the story of a friend who is dealing with a difficulty. Take the tape to your formal prayer time. Listen to it with God right beside you, and reflect on what is taking place. This technique, especially recording the stories of friends in need, gives verbal-linguistic people a chance to hear how they are perceiving a situation. Perhaps some prejudice is keeping you from responding in a positive way to your friend's situation. Perhaps your friend's situation reminds you of something that is happening in your life. Often new things will surface as you listen prayerfully to the tape. This type of prayer will offer new angles and insights that will identify areas in which you can give needed support, in which you might be contributing to the problem, or in which understanding is lacking.

• Write a new parable. Make or find a box that can be kept in your prayer area. Fill the box with favorite quotations, ad slogans, comments from friends and enemies—in short, anything that will spur your thinking. Choose an item from the box. Reflect on what you have chosen, then begin to write a parable about it. Remember that a parable is a story that teaches a lesson. What story can you write that will reveal something about God or your faith journey? Once you have finished writing, take the parable, sit down with God, and think about what it has to say about you, your life, and those around you. Talk over your insights with God. Keep these parables to help you reflect on your personal growth and faith journey in the years to come.

• "Mantra" comes from the Sanskrit for "instrument (tra) of reflection (man)." A mantra is a word or phrase that has power. Mantras have been used throughout the history of religion and serve to help people focus on God. Sometimes mantras are specific words and sometimes only a sound. The mantra doesn't express a thought, but serves to generate thoughts. In Christian tradition, the name of Jesus is often used as a mantra; a meaningful word or phrase, such as "hope" or "rejoice forever," is also appropriate. Settle in a quiet place and begin to say the word or phrase over and over, simply letting the words flow through you. If your mind begins to wander, gently return to the recitation.

• A variation on the mantra is to take a word or phrase and repeat it several times. Then say the words with as many different emotions as you find surfacing. Stay with one emotion for a bit and listen. Let the words float around you. Allow the images to come and the thoughts to surface. Let God work in you.

• Whispered prayer is also a good form for those strong in verbal-linguistic intelligence. Choose a psalm or other prayer, or write one of your own. Whisper the prayer, focusing on the words. Repeat it as often as you are inclined. Listen. End with a loud "Amen!"

• Ask people for their favorite prayers. You might even consider having them recite their prayer while you tape them. Later, in your own prayer reflection, listen to one of the prayers, think of the person and imagine why it is their favorite. Listen again, carefully reflecting on the words. Finally, thank God for the person who cared enough to share their prayer with you.

• Collect prayers from other people, perhaps taping them as they say the prayer. When you want to use this form of prayer, choose a prayer from one of these people, putting them before God and opening yourself to greater understanding.

• Use newspapers, television, and radio to pray. Watch, absorb, and remember that God is with you while you watch sitcoms, advertisements, or the news. What is God saying through this medium? After you've enjoyed the program or gotten upset at an advertisement, remember to talk to God, either aloud or in silence, and listen to God's response.

• Make your own distinctive prayer book. Use quotes that you find insightful or that remind you of an encounter with another that was significant for your spiritual life. Include favorite prayers or pictures of people that you want to remember in a special way. Like a memory album you make for your family and friends, this book can become an album about your relationship with God.

• Because I communicate better through writing, whenever I am upset or happy about something, I write about it. Even in my marriage, when things have to be said, I find that writing it first helps with the talking. The same thing applies to God. Write to God about your concerns, about your joys. Certainly, write love letters to God.

• Sometimes others say what we are trying to say but cannot

find the words for. At times such as these, the traditional prayers that fill books and stretch back over the years may be the best prayers for us. We can use those words to tell God what we are feeling. Remember to listen to God's side of the prayer, as the man at the beginning of the chapter did during the Our Father.

• Meditative reading is a good way to pray for those with strong verbal-linguistic intelligence. When you are embarking on this type of prayer encounter, choose an appropriate text to read. In addition to Scripture, there are many books which lend themselves readily to meditative reading. Carefully choose the time and the place where you will read. Make sure that others know this is your special time, as they might just mistake what you are doing for recreational reading. Read your selection through once. Think about what is being said and how it applies to your life. Talk with God about this, then re-read the section. Listen; pray. The significance of this time will grow as you become more accustomed to the ritual.

• In his spiritual exercises, St. Ignatius popularized the "you-are-there" approach to prayer reflection. He suggested re-creating scenes in our imaginations, even becoming someone in the story. This technique enables you to look at the main points of the story from a different perspective and see what they are calling you to do. Begin with choosing a story from Scripture, perhaps the account of feeding the five thousand or the wedding feast at Cana. Read the passage several times, then decide on whose character you want to adopt. You might also consider becoming some "thing," such as the wine jug at the wedding or the loaf of bread at the feeding of the five thousand. Imagine yourself as that person or thing. Feel the air around you, the people talking, the interactions you have. Let the time with God and your imagination lend new insights to your prayer.

• Some people with strong verbal-linguistic intelligence are able to "pray in tongues." If you want to try this approach, begin your formal prayer time by speaking out loud in your own language. Ask God to give you the gift of tongues. Become silent and wait for God to work in you. After a time you will find yourself welling over with the desire to express your love for God. Open your mouth and let the words come forth. They might not make sense and they might not be from a familiar language, but the expression of God's words will be enough. Pray them with confidence.

Using your verbal-linguistic intelligence when you encounter God enables you to engage your imagination and heart. It allows you to breathe life into flat words and create images that give depth and breadth to your friendship with God.

7

Praying with Logical-Mathematical Intelligence

If we have died with him, we will also live with him;
If we endure, we will also reign with him;
If we deny him, he will also deny us;
If we are faithless, he remains faithful—
for he cannot deny himself.

2 Timothy 2:11–13

All of us long for consistency. Parenting gurus talk about its importance in raising our children. Businesses want their earnings to grow steadily. The Church year is consistent in its feasts and Ordinary Time. Consistency keeps us grounded and helps us figure out problems when they arise. Logical-mathematical intelligence blossoms in an atmosphere of consistency and order. Within such an atmosphere, this intelligence can help us work out many aspects of faith.

Individuals who are strong in logical-mathematical intelligence love logical or numerical patterns and long chains of reasoning. They are able to connect different factors and see the relationship of one thing to another, arriving at a solution through sequential steps. When it comes to God, those with strength in this intelligence thrive on connections. And when those connections are made, the relationship with God is nurtured.

For those with strong logical-mathematical intelligence, the prayer of connections helps to nurture their logical mind as well as awaken them to the magical times of God's presence in their lives. How often, usually in hindsight, have you seen God working in your life? Through a prayer of connections we can easily begin to see how all of us are intertwined, how we all are members of God's family. And when this great truth begins to sink in, how can we continue to hurt one another?

Here is an example of a prayer of connections:

• Become aware of God right there with you. Take an object, any object, and begin to make connections. It is good to choose something from a place where you spend a lot of time, perhaps your kitchen, your office, or the garden. Suppose you choose a pencil. Think of the tree that the wood came from, the laborers who cut and fashioned it, store clerks who stocked it, and the first thing written with it. How does its shape relate to God? Does God have many sides? Does God offer us an eraser to remind us about forgiveness? Does God point us in the right direction? Use whatever connections come to you to consider what God is asking you to do and be at the present time.

The prayer of connections moves you to an encounter with God that brings a greater understanding of God, of yourself, and of others.

• Family photos offer an opportunity for connections. Take a picture and see who is in it. What exchanges have you had with that person? What did they teach you? What can they teach you today? What do they show you about God? Close your prayer by placing the person in the photo in the hands of God.

• Use books on saints and stories of people from all walks of life to make connections. The Communion of Saints is an important belief in the Catholic Church, and a great reminder of connections. Imagine that we are connected to such saintly figures as Francis of Assisi, Archbishop Oscar Romero, Catherine of Siena, and Bernadette of Lourdes! In prayer, I can talk to Francis about how uncomfortable I am when I see someone begging on the street, and if I listen, Francis will respond. I can talk to Oscar Romero about what it means to stand up for my faith, or ask Bernadette what it is like to be content with suffering. Through prayer and meditation I can make connections with each of these lives and others—including those of my family and friends who have died—who can teach me something about God, revealing a bit more of our Creator.

All Saints, by Robert Ellsberg, is a wonderful collection of daily reflections on saints, prophets, and witnesses for our time. Not all of those included in this book have been canonized, nor have all led exemplary lives, but each provides a reflection of God. For example, St. Bonaventure, who lived in the 1200s and was named a Doctor of the Church, is a great example of mediation. He tried to help the Franciscans steer a course between prayer and good works. He was also the saint who said, "A spiritual joy is the greatest sign of the divine grace dwelling within a soul." It is likely that Bonaventure was acquainted with Hildegard of Bingen, for he too speaks of the importance of being enthusiastic about our faith and our God.

Another helpful book, *The Birthday Book of Saints*, presents the lighter side of sainthood. These stories relate the faults and foibles of many known and unknown saints, and help us remember that we don't have to be perfect for God to love us. We just have to be ourselves and try as best we can to be the person God calls us to be. This book, like the previous one, calls us to make connections. One story tells of St. Vladimir, a Russian czar who had five wives and fifteen mistresses; but when his soul was touched by God, his life turned around. Another story tells of St. Dymphna, who had to ward off her father's advances, and finally died at his hands. These are people who struggled, yet who still were able to grow to grow in faith and love of God.

• The Internet is a great tool to use in making prayer connections. I realized this while selling an item on E-bay. After the auction was over, the person did not respond to my e-mails or pay for the item he had won at auction. A month after the non-transaction, I sent one last e-mail informing the person I would be re-listing the item. That evening I received an e-mail from him, apologizing for not contacting me and explaining all the crazy things that had taken place in his life during that month. I responded with understanding and received another e-mail saying that he really appreciated the contact, that no one seemed to have cared about his misfortune. He thanked me profusely for my understanding. That night I put him before God as I drifted off to sleep. Now, whenever I do an E-bay transaction or do research on the Internet or read my e-mail, I am conscious of the connectedness of our lives. It's the connection all of us have as children of God.

• For people with strong logical-mathematical intelligence, as well as for those with strong visual-spatial intelligence, a prayer of connections centered on making difficult decisions is good. Before your formal prayer time, gather several smal objects. Once you have done this, begin your time, as always, by becoming aware of God who is always with you. Now choose a story from Scripture or from the lives of saints where a difficult decision is involved. Consider the struggle of making a decision. Perhaps it was Jesus in the garden when he knew he was going to die, when he struggled to follow his father's will. Perhaps it was Mary as she responded to the Angel Gabriel concerning Jesus' coming. After you have had some time to reflect, look at the objects you chose and think of some decisions that are facing you. Focus on the decisions you must make, the choices that are at hand. Ask God to give you the wisdom to guide you as you deal with these decisions. Now choose one of the objects to carry with you in the coming week to serve as a constant reminder of God's presence and support as you make any kind of decision.

• Examination of conscience remains a very good logical-mathematical way of prayer. The examination of conscience has been around for a long time in the Church, but today it doesn't have the prominence it once did. In times past, it carried a lot of negativism which only served to make people fear God and not enter into loving relationships with the Creator. Today the examination of conscience can help us to learn not only what we are struggling with, but also to see the progress we have made in our lives. For those with strong logical-mathematical intelligence, it provides an opportunity to see the logical progression of spiritual growth and the areas in which we continue to need healing.

The examination of conscience doesn't have to be long and involved; a question or two a night would certainly be enough. Choose an area of your life that is troubling you. Become aware of God's love for you, and slowly begin to consider the ways in which you have failed. Consider also the ways in which you have grown during the past week, month, or year. List both your failures and your areas of growth if you feel it is helpful. Finally, look at them together with God. Let God pat you on the back for the areas of growth and listen to God's advice for what still needs to be done.

• Another connection prayer encounter for the logical-mathematical person is baking. I was first introduced to this through a recipe that used biblical references throughout. One had to look up the a particular Scripture passage to determine the ingredient, carefully putting together what turned out to be a fruit cake. Many recipes can be converted to Scripture references in this way. It just takes a bit of searching and creativity, both of which the person with strong logical-mathematical intelligence thrives on. Simply following a recipe can also be a prayerful encounter. According to Father Ed Hays, author of many books, we need to become aware of the sacred around us. Going about our daily work offers us a chance to reflect on God's goodness in providing us the food we eat, the clothes we wear, and the homes in which we live.

Individuals with strength in logical-mathematical intelligence like to explore relationships and patterns. They like to experiment with things they don't understand, to ask questions, and to look into problems in a well-ordered way. They pray best by looking for connections. Ultimately, since everything connects us with God, prayer opportunities abound for those with logical-mathematical intelligence.

8

Praying with Musical-Rhythmic Intelligence

I can only gaze at the universe in its full, true form,
At the millions of stars in the sky
carrying their huge harmonious beauty—
Never breaking their rhythm or losing their tune.

Rabindranath Tagore, Nobel Laureate for Literature

Even with his great military and political strength, King David of Old Testament fame was tender and poetic. Composer of a number of psalms, most likely he was a good musician, his musical prowess dating from his time as a shepherd. Musical-rhythmic intelligence was a great part of his life, and he used that intelligence regularly to praise his Maker, lament his wrongdoings, and allow his heart to spill over in gratitude.

Musical-rhythmic intelligence is the ability to produce and appreciate rhythm, pitch, and timbre, and to appreciate various forms of musical expression. This intelligence is also sensitive to the sounds of the environment and the human voice. In prayer encounters it is important for those with strong musical-rhythmic intelligence to use as many avenues of sound as possible.

Many day-to-day prayer possibilities abound for those with strength in musical-rhythmic intelligence.

• While watching television, listen to a commercial and have the jingle bring you into contact with God. What words must you change? What rhythms would be different? Consider the beauty of the song itself. What does it say to you about God?

• Everyone, no matter what the degree of their musical-rhythmic intelligence, has a favorite kind of music. Consider what your favorite type is and then make the connection to God. What does it say to you about God? How is God present in this particular type of music? (And, yes, God is present in hard rock!) Take this encounter a bit further. Write new lyrics for three or four songs familiar to you that could be used for a musical about one of the parables, or a particular teaching of Jesus, or something of significance you have read. Perform the piece for God.

• "Found" sounds are those already in a room, sounds made by the people in the room, or the hum of the refrigerator, or the scraping of feet on a rug. Use found sounds to express what you are feeling in your prayer. Gather together various objects, such as a musical instrument or a crumpled piece of paper, any thing that can make some type of sound. Become quiet and aware of God's presence. Realize how much you value God's friendship. Now consider something in your life. This might be something you are grateful for or something causing you pain. Whatever it is, listen and become aware of how you are reacting to this thought. Next, using the things you have gathered and your own humming, express what you are thinking and feeling. Express the emptiness you feel since your closest friend has moved out of the city, or your hope for what your relationship with God could become. Let the sounds and the rhythm flow freely. When you are done, become quiet and listen to the echoes of the rhythm and sound. Listen to the gathering silence, and hear how God responds.

• Found sounds can be used throughout the day to keep you in contact with God. Tap on your steering wheel when stopped at a red light and become aware of your heartbeat, which God makes possible. Listen to the sound of your feet as you walk along and reflect on how we are all called to journey in faith. Found sounds keep you aware of God with you.

• Express your prayer in motion and dance. Put on some music, use ribbons or scarves if you like, and dance for your Creator. Let the music speak, then let your body express what is in your heart. This kind of prayer can be energizing and affirming not only for those with musical-rhythmic intelligence, but also for those with strong bodily-kinesthetic intelligence.

• Think of something that is making you sad in your life. Many of us are dealing with what sometimes appear to be overwhelming challenges, yet we shy away from sharing these difficult times with God. Take time now to make up a song about this sadness—in effect, to sing the blues. When you are ready, sing your blues to God and always, always listen for the response.

• A good prayer encounter for those with strength in musical-rhythmic, bodily-kinesthetic, or verbal-linguistic intelligence is painting and/or writing a song. Get a paper and pencil, or if you prefer, paper and paints. Choose a song that speaks to you in some way. Sit down, pencil or paints in hand, and cue up the music. Close your eyes, listen, and begin to draw or paint as you feel the music move through you. Concentrate on God guiding your hand and on your heart supplying the subject. When you feel so inclined, begin to write what is coming to mind. Write whatever you are saying to God, and what God is saying to you. Write down your concerns, joys, whatever. When the music ends, take some time to re-read what you have written and talk it over with God.

• Drumming has been a form of prayer since ancient times. It is found in just about every culture and on every continent. The entire universe as God created it has a rhythm, and the world around us vibrates with that rhythm. Drumming was and is used to bring a focus to the physical rhythm of the world so that its intensity can be channeled into driving away worries and obsessive concerns. Drumming can make us more aware of God's presence. Get a drum and practice holding a beat, either alone or with accompanying music. Try to sustain the beat, concentrating on the sound. Let the drumming come to a natural end. Much like a mantra, drumming frees up the mind and allows God to work.

• For those with strong musical-rhythmic intelligence, it is important to integrate the rhythms of prayer into day-to-day life. One way to do this is during a session of meditative reading. Choose one short phrase or one word and repeat it again and again, being ever aware of God's presence. Let a melody emerge, and sing the melody over and over until it is fixed in your mind. Sing this song throughout the week, adding words if you like, letting it become as much an unconscious part of you as breathing.

• When we focus on our hearing, we are able to become more aware of the rhythms of life around us. Do you listen to the wind through the trees? In Scripture we are told that God is in the whisper of the wind. Have you heard God in this way?

One of the best ways I have found in which to use my musical intelligence in prayer is with my plants. During the spring, summer, and fall, our back porch is full of plants. Often when I go out to water them, I sit down on the porch and become quiet. I imagine the sound of the plants as they absorb the water, the sound of the plants as they grow, the sound of the wind fluttering through their leaves. Slowly my mind moves to a comparison of the plants' growth with my present spiritual growth. Am I struggling for water? Am I in need of nutrients? Am I shying away from the wind, away from God for some reason? Am I aware of the parts of my life that are growing, even though I don't realize it? The time of watering my plants then becomes a time of watering my soul.

Someone who has taken musical–rhythmic intelligence to a place of deep prayer is Theresa Schroeder-Sheker of Missoula, Montana. With her Chalice of Repose Project, she helps dying individuals leave this world amid music that matches their body rhythms. Theresa listens to their body rhythms as they near death, and then plays music to match their individual rhythm, allowing the music to accompany the person into heaven.

Using musical-rhythmic intelligence when we pray allows us to get in touch with the natural rhythm of life, the rhythm of God. It is a musical rhythm that will follow us throughout our mortal lives, and, as Theresa Schroeder-Sheker, believes, into eternal life.

9

Praying with Visual-Spatial Intelligence

I am circling and circling...
Am I a falcon, a storm, or a great song?

Rainer Maria Rilke

How many times have you been asked to choose your favorite color, your favorite activity, or your favorite music? Often the choice is intimately connected with how you see yourself. Choices like these give us a tangible way to express the intangibles in our being. This capacity is part of visual-spatial intelligence.

Visual-spatial intelligence involves pictures and images. It is present in people who can perceive the visual world accurately and then recreate their experience. They see form, color, shape, and texture in their mind's eye and are easily able to transfer those elements to concrete representations. For individuals with strong visual-spatial intelligence, it is important to use approaches in prayer that will enable concepts to take form.

• One particularly good prayer encounter for those with strong visual-spatial intelligence is to take a picture from a magazine or book and consider what it is saying to you about God. Take in all of the elements of the picture and let your thoughts flow, ever aware of God's presence beside you.

• The creation and use of symbols is a simple way to allow a concept to become concrete. Throughout the years, the Church has used symbols to assist in prayer and worship activities. The visual-spatial person might want to resurrect some of these prayer forms.

The Sign of the Cross. People with strong visual-spatial intelligence can grow in prayer by becoming more aware of what is implied by the sign of the cross. We often sign ourselves without any thought to what we are actually doing. Take the time to pay attention to how you are making the sign of the cross, then consider the words as you do so: "In the name of the Father, and of the Son, and of the Holy Spirit. Amen." Essentially, this prayer affirms that all we say or do is said and done in God's name. For those with strong visual-spatial intelligence (or for that matter, those with any of the intelligences), contemplation of the words and symbols of the sign of the cross can open many doors to God.

The Way of the Cross. Go to a church and walk slowly from station to station, reflecting on the visual depictions of Jesus' passion and death. Let yourself respond to these scenes. Don't feel that you have to pray at all the stations. Even reflecting on only one or two stations can help you open your heart to the passion of Jesus and consider the ways it relates to your own life.

Icons. These sacred pictures, originating in the Eastern Orthodox Church, are excellent visuals aids to prayer. Icons are considered to be the product of the Holy Spirit inspiring the hands of the artists. They are often referred to as "windows to heaven," and represent many theological truths. To use an icon in prayer, gaze at the icon. Take everything in. Who does the icon depict? What are the symbols present in the painting? What does the icon say to you? Often you will find the message so clear that the icon literally "speaks."

At one time, I was not very fond of icons. But one day, Mary Kay Meyer, director of Shalom Catholic Worker House in Kansas City, gave me an icon of Juan Diego as a gift. I took it, although I wasn't sure what I would do with it. I finally decided to experiment with it in my formal prayer time. (God always teaches me something I am not expecting when I experiment!) I sat down and stared at the icon. Juan had his arms outstretched, and his feet were spread outward, almost as if his whole body was bent on evangelization. The image of the Virgin was on his robe. There Juan stood, looking at me. His eyes probed deep within me. I wanted to look away but couldn't. I started to cry.

I knew from history that the Aztec people had been dehumanized by their European conquerors and alienated from the Catholic Church as well. On December 9, 1531, Mary appeared to Juan Diego as an Aztec woman and spoke to him in Nahuatl, the Aztec tongue, using the manner one would use to address royalty. She appeared in the hills outside of Mexico City, the center of Spanish power. Mary's appearance, I think, was God's way of restoring the dignity of the Aztec people.

The more I stared at the icon, the more I realized that too

often the Church alienates its members. Yet it is often these marginalized people who have the gifts the Church needs in order to grow. I began to wonder what gifts others have tried to give me that I rejected. Who had *I* marginalized? I left this prayer time with a new insight about the power of using images for prayer.

In praying this way, the image you use does not have to be an icon. You can use artwork or photographs. Whatever you use, let the image speak to you. Individuals with strong visual-spatial intelligence, as well as those with bodily-kinesthetic intelligence, will feel right at home doing this. Those strong in other intelligences might have to stretch themselves but the experience is well worth it. There is power in images, and that power can draw us closer to God.

• Along with resurrecting symbols in your life, you can create symbols of your own to remind you of the truths of faith. For example, cross two band-aids to symbolize the healing power of Christ.

• Another very simple approach for those with strong visual-spatial intelligence is to use a scarf in prayer. Knot one end, then think of everything God has given you, changing the shape of the knot to reflect your thoughts.

• If you have access to slides, prepare a slide show that depicts what is in your heart, what is troubling you, or what you want to say to God. Show it to yourself or others—this prayer exercise is good for all the intelligences—and meditate on the goodness of God.

• The beneficial use of candles in prayer is often overlooked. Fire is a significant symbol in many faiths, both in the East and in the West. To use candles during a prayer encounter, find a safe and quiet place. Light the candle and sit in front of it. Look into the flame, watching its colors change, its size increase and decrease. Become aware of God, of the power of the light. Feel yourself in God's light. Spend some time being silent with God. When you are done with your meditation, blow out the candle.

You may also want to light a candle during dinner as a reminder of the sacredness of mealtime.

• Another simple prayer image is a small box kept on the kitchen table or in another prominent place. Every time you go out to dinner, place an amount equal to the cost of one serving in the box. Perhaps monthly or less, gather the money and send it to an organization that helps people who are hungry. This simple act is a sign of our connection with the world and reminds us to pray for people in need.

• Transformation takes place in our everyday lives. As we grow more and more in our spirituality, we find ourselves coming out of our cocoons and blossoming into butterflies who grow more and more beautiful each day. We turn away from our old ways of behaving and of relating to God, and put on the new clothes of awakened awareness. In so doing, we open the door for God to do even greater things in our lives.

I remember the first day after I hit rock bottom during a personal crisis. I was walking to the store and one line kept running through my head: "Nothing will ever be the same again." This is true whenever we move toward God: nothing will ever be the same again. Our lives will be transformed. Our old habits will change into new ones as we work each day to follow God's path.

For individuals with strong visual-spatial intelligence, one of the best ways to become aware of the transformations in their lives is to do something concrete to symbolize the transformation inside. This may mean creating a picture, or writing a story, or sculpting in clay—anything that will symbolize the change that has taken place. During this crisis, my husband wrote me a letter in which he told me how much he loved me. He wrote that I had to make a choice, but that he would continue to love me no matter what, even if he had to leave. That letter became a symbol of my transformation and to this day it brings back the flood of emotions from those early days when my wings were just beginning to dry.

Our church tradition is rich in symbols; reawaken this tradition in your own life. What symbol can you use for your transformation?

• For those strong in visual-spatial intelligence, beauty is a great factor in their prayer. Father Matthew Fox says this: "Beauty saves. Beauty heals. Beauty motivates. Beauty unites. Beauty returns us to our origins and here lies the ultimate act of saving, of healing, of overcoming dualism. Beauty allows us to forget the pain and dwell on the joy." Beauty helps visual-spatial learners deepen their prayer experiences.

• Beauty is an important element in the celebration of Mass, and those strong in visual-spatial intelligence can be valuable contributors to enhancing the environment for liturgy. This can mean paying attention to the colors on the altar or to the position of various objects in the sanctuary. It might mean arranging the flowers in the church or choosing appropriate wall hangings. All of these gestures can be a prayer experience for those strong in visual-spatial intelligence.

• Make your own prayer space at home. Joseph Campbell, student of myth, said a sacred space should be a place where wonder can be revealed. Here you can get in touch with the divine who is larger than you. Let your sacred space reflect who you are and who you are trying to become. Make rich use of symbols that carry meaning for you. Fill your space with what will delight the senses: light, scent, color, words, and music.

Visual-spatial people can see the unseen. They find it easier to make a leap of faith, to pray, when they are able to make a connection between the picture in their mind and the concrete. In his book, *The Little Prince*, Antoine Saint-Exupéry writes, "It is only with the heart that one can see rightly; what is essential is invisible to the eye." These words well describe the prayer experience for those strong in visual-spatial intelligence.

10

Praying with Bodily-Kinesthetic Intelligence

Hands to work, hearts to God.

Shaker saying

Kansas is known as the Land of Oz, but in a new promotion for the state, it became the Land of "Ahs," calling people to remember all the breathtaking sights the state has to offer.

We all need "ahs" in our lives. These are the moments when God is most fully alive to us. We find our "ah" in the dream that sheds insight into an aspect of our life, or in the moment when we see clearly what direction we are to take. It is the mysterious connection we make with God through a reading, a person, or a particular incident. The "ahs" in our lives are the times when God is being made manifest in a very real, very concrete way— if we only open our eyes. Our vision and our "ahs" are connected; one cannot happen without the other.

The persons with strong bodily-kinesthetic intelligence finds the "ahs" in the tastes, smells, and sounds of the world. They feel it in the movements of their bodies and the creations all around them. They savor the incense burned at liturgy. They let the juice of the grape awaken their taste buds. Bodily-kinesthetic intelligence needs and uses the total body for expression.

• One of the best ways for those strong in this intelligence to pray is through dance and movement. Consider choreographing a well-known passage from Scripture, and perform it for God.

• Because dance is an expression of feeling, it is a wonderful means of prayer. If you are too self-conscious about dancing, try clapping, jumping, swaying, turning, bending, or pointing. Anything that involves the body is a way to give praise and connect to God through bodily-kinesthetic intelligence.

• Imagine that you are broadcasting the Good News on the radio. What would you do? What would you say? Take time to actually put together a radio program. Include time to interview God or a favorite saint. After you finish the program, spend time in reflection.

• Dance enables us to use our entire being to communicate with God. Create a dance to show what you are feeling at the moment: a sense of awe at the greatness of God, sorrow for a loss, a need for help, or gratefulness for something or someone. Choose something to wear during the dance. Decide on what music you will use and whether or not you will sing. Finally, become aware of God's presence and dance your heart out before your Creator.

• As she speaks to groups throughout the country, Sr. Jose Hobday, often shares this prayer, which her mother taught her when she was quite young. It is called the "hug prayer," and it is good not only for those strong in bodily-kinesthetic intelligence, but also for those with strong intrapersonal intelligence. Here is what you do:

Put your arms around yourself. Cuddle your body. Hold yourself like you would hold a baby. Once you have a good hold of yourself, close your eyes and begin to rock. Keep doing it. While doing this, remember that you are God's child, and that God understands you and holds you close, just as you are holding yourself, because God loves you very much.

• Many of us have allowed our bodies to go fallow. We don't run or jump or dance or skip as we might have done while growing up. Maybe we are dealing with a physical challenge that keeps us from being active. No matter what our physical condition, however, we can awaken our bodies in prayer through our fingers. To do so, flex your fingers and become aware of the gift God has given you in fingers. Notice the wrinkles and calluses, the nails and cuticles, how they bend or refuse to bend. Now look at your hands. Call to mind St. Teresa of Avila's admonition that "Christ has no hands but yours." Slowly let your hands move in response to your thoughts, to the conversation you are having with God. Let them express how they feel about being instruments of the Lord's work. Let them tap out your thoughts; let them feel God's presence.

This prayer can be done anywhere, at anytime. Do it while washing dishes, while weeding the garden, or while typing at the computer. Use your hands to celebrate the God who asks you to carry on Christ's work upon earth.

• Make a simple yeast bread. Gather all the ingredients and utensils together. Include some rolled oats and a mortar and pestle. Put your work before God. Begin by using the mortar and pestle to grind the oats to the consistency of flour, then add the bread ingredients to the oats. As you knead the bread, think of the ways in which you have been shaped since your birth. Remember how you were formed in your mother's womb; remember times growing up that were significant for you. Remember the times when you felt God's presence in your life.

As you leave the bread for its first rising, sit in a chair and remember the times when you felt God was not present in your life. Become aware of all your dark moments. With God at your side, peer through the darkness and see how God was at work in your life even if you felt differently. As you punch down the dough, remember the things you had to knock out of your life in order to grow. As you shape the loaf, think of the new growth occurring in your life right now and the ways in which God is present to you. During the second rising, contemplate the times in your life when you were resurrected, when you rose to new levels. As the bread bakes, savor its smells. Finally, when the bread is done, cut a slice and savor the goodness, remembering as you do that Jesus is the bread of life.

• A good prayer practice for those strong in bodily-kinesthetic intelligence is the practice of Zen walking. This is perhaps one of the simplest and yet most difficult prayer experiences. To do it, you just walk; it is that simple, yet that difficult. Begin by standing still and centering yourself. Do not take the first step until all your urge to move is gone. Lift your right foot; become aware of your heel leaving the ground, of the ball of the foot moving upward, of your toes moving. Wait until you feel no urge to move on, then put your foot down. Move as slowly as you can without losing your balance, and move only after all urges to move have passed. Pay attention to how your hips move, how your weight shifts. With each move become ever more aware of the God who empowers you.

Different regions and cultures have different body customs for prayer. Several denominations in the United States hold hands while praying. On the other hand, the Quakers do not touch but rather sit in silence, waiting for the Spirit. People from some cultures take off their shoes before praying, while others emphasize quiet, conscious eating. Many cultures encourage dance as a means of communication with the divine, especially in African-American churches, where movement of the whole body is emphasized.

At the Incarnation, God became human in the person of Jesus. God took on a body and it was good. As recounted in the gospels, Jesus climbed hills, walked on water, slept, cried, feasted at the wedding in Cana, and wrote in the sand. The parables are replete with physical activity—sweeping the house, looking for lost coins, guarding pigs, kneading dough, eating fish. And in 1 Corinthians 6:19, St. Paul writes: "Do you not know that your body is a temple of the Holy Spirit within you, which you have from God…?"

To pray with the body is to really know and appreciate your body. It is a special gift to God. The Song of Songs speaks deeply and prayerfully about the body:

How beautiful you are, my love, how very beautiful! Your eyes are doves behind your veil. Your hair is like a flock of goats, moving down the slopes of Gilead. Your teeth are like a flock of shorn ewes that have come up from the washing, all of which bear twins, and not one among them is bereaved. Your lips are like a crimson thread, and your mouth is lovely. Your cheeks are like halves of a pomegranate behind your veil (Song of Songs 4:1–3).

Wow! What a love song! God made us both beautiful and wonderful, and there is no better way to express our love for the Creator than to use our gifts in some way.

Matthew Fox begins his book on creation theology with the words, "In the beginning was joy." If we become complacent in our faith, our joy disappears and apathy takes its place. In order to resurrect that joy, we might want to try praying with bodily-kinesthetic intelligence. Prayer should make you sweat!

The body is such a great gift, one that we too often ignore. Take time in your prayer to consider how wonderfully it is made. Julian of Norwich said, "God does not despise creation nor does God disdain to save us in the simplest function that belongs to our bodies." Every part of our bodies was created by God. Wonder and rejoice in this marvelous gift!

11

Praying with Naturalist Intelligence

Invite the sacred to participate in your joy in little things, as well as in your agony over the great ones. There are as many miracles to be seen through a microscope as through a telescope. Start with the little things seen through the magnifying glass of wonder, and just as a magnifying glass can focus the sunlight into a burning beam that can set a leaf aflame, so can your focused wonder set you ablaze with insight.

Alice Howell, artist

My mother loved flowers and was always planting something new in the yard. In an effort to keep the eight of us out of her flower beds, she designated a small section of the yard where we could dig to our hearts content. Hours were spent there digging to China, building towns, and watching; yes, watching. Watching ants invade our hole; watching worms as they ran from the bright sunlight; and watching larvae curl into balls. That hole gave all of us an opportunity to be in touch with the wonderful world God had given us. It was the beginning of nurturing our naturalist intelligence.

Naturalist intelligence is sensitivity to the natural world. Most people graced with a strong naturalist intelligence have a keen ability to recognize and categorize plants, animals, and other objects in nature. They consider how nature interacts with itself and with humankind.

• The naturalist intelligence lends itself to the creation of ritual because rituals often carry within them the rhythm of life, the ebb and flow of classification. Take some time for creating a ritual. What might that include?

• Consider with God the steps you need to take to grow as a Christian. List them and look at what areas of your life are involved.

• Remember when you were little and you would spend time just looking at clouds? Remember all the different things you could see in the clouds? Take a cloud trip today. Let your imagination run wild as you stare at the clouds. Imagine anything. Allow yourself to become aware of God watching the clouds with you. What thoughts arise? Talk with God about all that you imagine. And remember that "having your head in the clouds" can be a very good thing.

An Alphabet of Grace

Frederick Buechner, a Presbyterian minister, talks about the "alphabet of grace." He says that life itself can be thought of as an alphabet through which God's presence and our purpose are revealed. Buechner says,

God speaks to us in such a way, presumably, not because he chooses to be obscure but because, unlike a dictionary word whose meaning is fixed, the meaning of an incarnate word is the meaning it has for the one it is spoken to, the meaning that becomes clear and effective in our lives only when we ferret it out for ourselves.

This is true of any of the multiple intelligences, but it's especially true for the naturalist intelligence, since that intelligence works directly with nature to discover the mysteries of God. The alphabet of grace speaks of taking ordinary, day-to-day activities and hearing what God is saying to us in them.

• Choose something, such as a leaf, a flower, or a shell, from the natural world. Close your eyes and touch it. Keep your eyes closed as you become familiar with it. Learn everything you can about this object through your senses before considering what God might be saying about it, and what significance might be attached to it. Ask God to show you what you can learn from this object of the world, this object of nature. Appreciate God's creation and give thanks.

• Another good prayer encounter for those with strong naturalist intelligence is a creation meditation. I don't know the origin of the meditation, but many years ago someone gave me a copy of it. This meditation is also very suitable for groups.

Beforehand, record the meditation (as on pages 75–76), so it can play without interruption while you pray. Be sure to pause for an adequate amount of time to allow for reflection. To begin, put a cup of water and a cup of soil in front of you. Become aware of God right there beside you. Feel the soil and the water, study their textures and consistencies. Now close your eyes. Concentrate as the words are spoken, giving thanks as you are so moved.

(Spoken text): When God began creating the heavens and the earth, God said, "Let there be light." And light appeared. Thank God for light. What if you lived in darkness? Picture the face of someone you dearly love—a friend, a parent, a child. Let that face now melt away into darkness. What if you lived in the soul of darkness always? Thank God for light. (Reflect)

And God said, "Let the vapors separate to form the sky above and the oceans below." Do you take water for granted? What if you should run out of it? Imagine yourself hot and thirsty. You take a glass of ice cold water. Imagine it going down your throat and quenching your thirst. Appreciate it for a moment. All of life depends upon it. Thank God for water. (Reflect)

Then God said, "Let the water beneath the sky be gathered into oceans so that dry land will emerge." Do you take soil for granted? Imagine the things you eat that come from the soil. Vegetables. Fruits. Imagine the flowers that come from the soil. What if we should pollute all of it? Could we exist? Thank God for soil. (Reflect)

Then God said, "Let there be bright lights in the sky to give light to the earth and to identify the day and the night; they shall bring about the seasons on the earth and mark the days and years." What if the seasons never changed? What if it were always winter? Picture your yard at home with no flowers, no leaves on the trees, no green bushes—not just for a few months out of the year, but for the whole year long. Thank God for seasons. (Reflect)

Then God said, "Let the waters team with fish and other life, and let the skies be filled with birds of every kind."

Thank God for birds. They teach us to soar. Picture yourself as a gliding seagull. Fly as high or as far as you want. Thank God for birds. (Reflect)

And God said, "Let the earth bring forth every kind of animal—cattle and reptiles and wildlife of every kind. And so it was." Thank God for animals. Imagine the animals that give you nourishment. Cattle and chickens and fish. Imagine the animals that give you pleasure. Your pet dog or cat or bird. Imagine all the different kinds of animals in the world. What would the world be like without animals? Thank God for animals. (Reflect)

Then God said, "Let us make man and woman—someone like ourselves, to be the masters of all life upon the earth and in the skies and in the seas. So God made man and woman." Thank God for you. Do you appreciate yourself with all your uniqueness, with all your special gifts and talents? Thank God for all the people in your life: your mother and father, your brothers and sisters, friends and enemies. Imagine life without other people: the aloneness, the lack of variety, the absence of love. Thank God for people. (Reflect)

Dear God, thank you for all your creation. Help me never to take it for granted. *(End of spoken text)*

• Perhaps one of the best encounters with the divine for those strong in naturalist intelligence is to undertake a pilgrimage. Pilgrimage is defined as a journey to a holy place or a search for an exalted purpose. All that is asked of the pilgrim is that he or she be open, attentive, and responsive. A pilgrimage can involve a walk through the neighborhood, simply being mindful that God is at our side. It could be a journey to visit a shrine, a church or churches, or some other religious place. It can also be an interior journey taken over a period of time; to do so, we may use a retreat setting or work with a spiritual adviser. Long or short, interior or exterior, the idea of pilgrimage is to reach a sacred point, whether in reality or in spirit.

To undertake a pilgrimage, decide first what your goal will be as you journey: a better understanding of your faith?; a deeper insight into God's love? Deal with the different people you encounter and the things that come your way. Take in your surroundings. Reflect. Be with God. Ask questions, and listen for the answers. Your first journey may not yield anything, nor may the second or third, but the joy is in the quest, in the search, in the gift of the company of God.

• Nature sketching is a good prayer experience for those with strong naturalist intelligence as well as those with visual-spatial intelligence. Frederick Franck, a painter, sculptor, and visionary, wrote of his art, "One day I realized that the seeing and the drawing had fused into one single individual act....It changed my life." Sketching nature can give us a powerful encounter with God that is beyond understanding.

Gather all your drawing equipment and find a good subject. Before starting to draw, observe carefully: the shapes around you, the colors, the negative space. Take in everything. Begin drawing, and let yourself get caught up in your work. Concentrate only on what you are drawing. Remember that God is there too, watching and sitting with you. Don't hurry. Rest in the art and rest in God. The understanding will come.

• With gardening, there is a connection with the earth that cannot be denied. For people with naturalist intelligence, gardening can be an experience of continuing spiritual growth. If you do not already have a garden in which to work, choose a section of your yard to begin. Use only hand tools to turn the soil, and natural products to enrich it. Plant vegetables or flowers. Tend to them lovingly, ever-mindful of being a co-creator with God. Avoid comparisons with other people's gardens, and don't moan about your tomatoes being too small or your pansies too spindly.

• One of the simplest ways for those with naturalist intelligence to encounter God is to walk. Walk slowly. Notice the life around you. Notice yourself as part of that life cycle. Let God hold you and the world in his hands. (You may also want to use the practice of Zen walking described on page 69.)

People with naturalist intelligence are in love with nature. Given the right opportunities, nature can help them fall deeper in love with the Creator.

12

Praying with Interpersonal Intelligence

A true friend unbosoms freely, advises justly, assists readily,
adventures boldly, takes all patiently, defends courageously
and continues a friend unchangeably.

William Penn

One evening, as we were bidding friends good-bye following supper together, the phone rang. Our son Nathaniel answered. I heard, "Hi, Jon. How's it going?" and I knew it was his friend of many years, Jon Sullivan. The next words out of Nathaniel's mouth stopped me in my tracks. "Don't worry, Jon," he said. "We'll be right there." Hanging up the phone, Nathaniel turned to us and said, "Jon's father was killed in an accident. We have to go. He needs us." Without hesitation and any further conversation, we were out the door and on the road to the Sullivan home.

It was a difficult time, but one of the thoughts that helped me through it was the fact that my son did not hesitate to respond to his friend's need. Fear of how to handle the situation, fear of the unknown didn't enter into his response. He just knew his friend needed help, and he responded to that need. This was his interpersonal intelligence coming through.

People with strong interpersonal intelligence have the ability to detect and respond appropriately to the moods, motivations, and desires of others. They are in harmony with other people. They have the ability to work cooperatively in a group as well as the ability to communicate both verbally and nonverbally with others. Group prayer encounters are very good for those with strong interpersonal intelligence.

• One of the best prayers for those strong in interpersonal intelligence, much like those with logical-mathematical intelligence, is the prayer of connections. Search out a picture of a bridge. Look at the ways the bridge connects. Consider ways in which you are a bridge and how you connect the people in your life. What part does God have in it all? Discuss this with God.

• Create a chant to describe what you are feeling for someone and take that chant before God.

• People with interpersonal intelligence should consider celebrating important rituals together with others. This would certainly include gatherings for Christmas or birthdays or graduations, as well as other occasions. In each of the thirty-three years we have been married, my husband, Ed and I have had a Paschal meal at our home. This is a combination of the Seder supper and the Last Supper, and includes many of the ritual foods from both of those meals. As mother, I have the privilege of lighting the festival lights. As I light the candles and recite the prayer, I feel a connection with the hundreds of thousands of people who have uttered that same prayer: "Blessed are you, O Lord, our God, King of the universe, who has made us holy by your commandments and enabled us to light the festival lights. Blessed are you, O Lord, our God, King of the universe, who has kept us alive and sustained us and brought us to this season."

• Another prayer experience for those with strong interpersonal intelligence is the blessing cup. We have a special cup which is always within view in our dining room and is brought to the table on special occasions. At these times, we use the book *The Blessing Cup* by Rock Travnikar, OFM, to celebrate the various occasions together with God. These rituals connect us to all those who share similar celebrations and remembrances. It brings home how, though all unique, we are also so much alike, sharing the same joys and sorrows and struggles for growth.

• Begin a prayer chain by cutting several strips of paper. Have the strips readily available throughout your house or workplace. Whenever someone or something comes to mind, write or draw it on the paper. Begin to make a chain that will grow as you become more aware of others in your prayer life. Keep the chain growing and visible so you remember your connection to others.

• Have a chair that is always empty, even when you have guests. Let it serve as a reminder that Christ must always be welcomed, regardless of what form he takes. Let it serve as a reminder of the love you have yet to give, of the hope you have yet to nurture, and of the faith you have yet to grow. In the Polish tradition, there is always an empty chair at meals during Christmas for greeting the Christ who might come to the door during that holy season. In the Jewish faith, an empty chair is set at the seder meal for Elijah. Let an empty chair be a symbol for you of God's presence everywhere around you.

• Choose a Scripture passage, perhaps one in which Jesus is talking to people. Now read the passage, but insert your name every so often. Also insert the name of someone you want to keep before God. Listen to the words; God is speaking directly to you.

• Interpersonal intelligence helps people nurture a relationship with God through the practice of compassion, which comes from the heart. When we reach out to people in compassion, we can often feel their pain. Compassion can be deepened through prayer. One way to do this is to take a stack of newspapers and magazines. Page through them thoughtfully, clipping pictures or stories that speak to you of the needs of others. Study these clippings, taking these people into your heart. Listen as God helps you find the best way to respond to them. Allow God to bring one particular situation to you. Love the person together with God; with the mind of God try to relate to what they may be feeling. See what God loves in that person.

• Too often, we think that if we are to respond with compassion, we have to *do* something. That is not always the case. Often, placing a person in God's hands is the greatest loving act we can do. When we do so, we are helping this person in the best way possible, by giving them to their Creator, who knows what is best for them.

• Another way to practice compassion is through "loving kindness," which means acting in accord with all the essential aspects of compassion. It is a practice that calls us to see the good in other people, yet not to ignore hurtful things. To pray in this way, first become aware of your own goodness. Use as a guide the second great commandment of Jesus, that is, to love your neighbor as yourself. By becoming aware of your own essential goodness, you will be given the strength to do good for others. Next, recall someone who loved you in a way that made you feel wonderful and really helped you. Who has been kind to you in your life? Remember them, and let that memory fill you with gratitude. If you have never felt the unconditional love of another, imagine a person who gives you unconditional love and imagine that you have received that love from that person. Feel yourself being filled with that love, and with God's love. When you are ready, let the love you have received flow to another person.

This practice is particularly helpful when you do not know how to help someone who is suffering. Imagine what you would feel if you were feeling the same pain. This will give you an awareness of what the other person may be going through, and also surface some possible ways to assist.

When my first child, Nathaniel, went off to Oberlin College, I didn't know what to expect. He was on his own, a thousand miles away. I worried about the experiences he would encounter, about drugs and alcohol and sex—everything news reporters tell you to worry about. I remembered my own college experiences, and hoped that my son would not have to go through the same confusion, temptations, and difficulties as I had. Finally, I reached a point where everyone around me became fed up with my constant worrying—probably even God, I thought.

Still, I could not stop worrying. Then one day as I was

praying, Nathaniel kept coming up as someone to place before God. I kept dismissing this and tried concentrating on finding someone else. But Nathaniel kept coming back into my heart. Finally, I realized that God was telling me something. (I'm a slow learner.)

So I took Nathaniel and loved him before God. I loved him as I imagined him at Oberlin going through a day. I loved him as I imagined him in different situations. I loved him as I pictured him alone and hurting. I loved him as I imagined him having a good time. And finally, I was moved to place him in God's hands. Lovingly, as only a mother can, I entrusted this child to God.

As I did, a thought came with crushing force: God loves Nathaniel more than I could ever hope to. He will be all right. I can't say that from that moment on I never worried about Nathaniel again, but I worried far, far less, and I drew comfort from the knowledge of the strength of God's love for him.

The Quakers speak of "holding someone in the light" as an expression of love. I now understand what that means.

When we nurture our prayer life by using our interpersonal intelligence, we nurture not only ourselves but the total community, as we grow ever more aware of the connection between God and each of us. "We were all created at the same time," says Julian of Norwich, "and in our creation we were knit and 'oned' to God."

At that creation, we were connected as closely as stitches in a sweater, each of us separate but essential for the total creation.

13

Praying with Intrapersonal Intelligence

Be still, and know that I am God!

Psalm 46:10

When my mother died, rather than flying, I chose to take an overnight train from Kansas City to Cleveland. I wanted time to think, to grapple with the fact that even though I was thirty-nine-years old, I was now an orphan. I spent the train trip thinking of death and life, of my memories of a woman who tried her best to raise eight children with little money or family support. I remember thinking that the reality of death adds a poignancy to life, and reminds us of how precious and how fleeting life is. This train ride to reflect on and celebrate my mother's life was God's gift to me. Here my intrapersonal intelligence would be challenged to help me grow through that moment in time.

People with strong intrapersonal intelligence know themselves. They know their feelings and emotional responses and are often given to self-reflection. They have a great sense of the spiritual, and look at the deeper picture not readily seen. Prayer experiences for those strong in this intelligence can be full of both struggle and insight.

• Taking on the identity of people from Scripture is a great way for those with intrapersonal intelligence to pray. Choose someone from Scripture or from another spiritual book. Take some time to "become" that person. Think about what they might have thought, and feel what they might have felt. Consider how they might have prayed. Become aware of God, then pray as the person you have chosen might have prayed. Close your time with God by praying as only you can.

• Cut out several comic strips from the Sunday paper and white out the dialogue bubbles. During your prayer time, use the comic strips to re-create the story shown in the strip. Fill in the bubbles to illustrate the new story you have imagined.

• Choose someone from the New Testament and reflect on what he or she might have learned from Jesus. Talk it over with God, and decide what this exercise means for your life.

• Find a special blanket or rug. This will become your prayer mat. Pull it out when you want to have a special encounter with God. You might liken it to dressing up for a date. Spread out your mat, then simply sit or lie or kneel on it in whatever way is comfortable for you. Become quiet and listen. What is God saying to you? Fully absorb God during this time. Acknowledge what God has done for you. Let God love you. Above all, simply be quiet and rest in God. And if you fall asleep, don't be too hard on yourself—after all, resting in the Lord can sometimes mean sleep.

• Guided imagery is another good prayer opportunity for those strong in intrapersonal intelligence. First find a story that appeals to you, preferably one with spiritual overtones. Tape the story, and then play the tape during your formal prayer time. Become quiet and center on God's presence. Listen as the story is read. Imagine yourself there, experiencing it right as it is happening. At the end, pause and listen for God's words. There are several books available that can help you in this process, in particular, *Imagine That*, by Marlene Halpin. You can also create your own stories, challenging your verbal-linguistic intelligence in the process.

• A one-word prayer can sometimes speak volumes. One word can express a deep feeling, whether happiness or sorrow. It is summoned from the depths of the person's soul. Use this type of prayer as you would a mantra (see page 44).

• The practice of mindfulness, while helpful for all the intelligences, is especially so for those with strong intrapersonal intelligence. Mindfulness is a state of awareness where you pay attention to the present moment. To practice mindfulness, choose a quiet place and time during your day. Close your eyes; pay attention to your body and any sensations that come, especially noting your breath and the sounds you hear. As thoughts come, you need only acknowledge them and then let them go, returning to the awareness of your breathing and the sensations around you. In doing so, you will become more aware of God's presence.

Mindfulness can be practiced throughout the day. When you awake, note something in your bedroom that will remind you of the present moment. Pay attention as you brush your teeth. Feel the coffee as it goes down your throat. Be present to the people you encounter. Mindfulness is difficult but it is a practice that brings us more closely in touch with God.

• One of the ways to further your relationship with God is to keep a dream journal. Dreams can give you clues, thoughts, and feelings that you might not be aware of. Dreams are another door to learning more about ourselves and about God. Begin to open the door by writing down your dreams upon awakening. Through this simple action, gradually you will find you are dreaming more and more. Pay attention to the dreams. Take one of your dreams into your quiet prayer time with God. Read what you have written about the dream, try to recreate it, then be still and listen. Gradually insights will dawn and your prayer will shed light on the meaning of the dream. Sometimes you will find that the dreams are just a way to release thoughts and feelings not expressed during the day. Other times you will find that certain problems in your life are being worked out in your dreams. Still other dreams will give you great insight into yourself.

One recurring dream of mine is about a house. The first time I had this dream was during a time of self-hatred and negativity in my life. The house looked okay on the outside, but once I went inside I discovered it was a one-room shack with walls rotting in certain places, broken windows, and garbage all over the floor. There was a door that led to another room but I was unable to open it.

Over the next few months, I kept having the same dream. But as I came to a better place in my life, and began to accept and love myself, I found that I was able to open the door and go into two larger rooms, which were cleaner and filled with all sorts of items, including a large grand piano. Again, there was a door which I was unable to open. As I learned more about myself and my relationship with God and others, I found meaning in the items in the room and I could once again open the next door. The house is now full of many rooms, each in a different stage of decoration. Some of the rooms I cannot yet enter, including a bedroom that I can see from the base of the steps.

For me, this dream represents my person. When I was in the depths of hating myself, the one-room shack surfaced. But as I learned more about myself and came to love and accept myself, I was able to open doors and discover new surprises awaiting me. Always in the dream was the loving presence of someone who, as the years went by, I came to know as God.

• Journaling is a time-honored practice that is part of many people's prayer lives. Journaling enables us to put down the feelings and thoughts we have as we travel along our path in life. Different from a diary, which records daily occurrences, a journal includes thoughts and feelings and insights. In short, it is a record of our spiritual growth. While important for all the intelligences (those with strong visual-spatial intelligence can do it in pictures), a journal is especially important for those with intrapersonal intelligence. It enables them to consider who they are, where they are going, and where God is in their lives. It provides an arena for insights and questions.

Before you begin to write, invite God to write along with you. Pause as you write to listen to what surfaces. Include these thoughts in your journal. Explore a particular experience or encounter with questions such as these: what touched me, and why? How was my perspective changed by this experience? Where did I see God in this encounter? Addressing these three areas will enable you to explore an encounter or experience with greater depth. As you complete your journal entry, thank God for being present. Periodically invite God to sit down with you and read your journal. Ask for openness to see where you have grown and where you have remained stuck. Consider what you will do to change a rigid behavior. Ask for God's help in taking steps to change.

• Another prayer experience is the exercise of writing an ethical will to be read upon your death. This type of will lists the values held dear by you and the persons to whom you would like to pass on these values. Write the will during prayer, asking God to be with you as you consider what you value in life and what you believe. Seal the ethical will and put it with your important papers. As the years pass, re-read it with God and see if what you believe has remained the same. Make sure that the ethical will is part of your funeral celebration.

• There is a type of prayer I have used to help me better understand myself in relation to others. It is a difficult prayer because it calls me to look closely at how I behave toward others, and to consider how I must change. To pray this way, begin, as always, by recognizing God's presence with you. Now, place before yourself and God a person with whom you don't get along. Ask yourself the question: what can I learn from this person? Answering that question will mean looking at the person, considering his or her strengths and talents, and reflecting on what you can learn from him or her. Draw the prayer to a close by putting the person and yourself before God.

The hard part is this: when you are with this particular person, listen to him or her carefully, resisting the urge to argue. Instead say the words, "You may be right." A tiny moment of humility may help you learn a big lesson of love.

As you grow in your prayer life by using your intrapersonal intelligence, you will find that the knowledge and insights you gain from God surface again and again to guide your behavior and decisions. You will come to know yourself better; that's what using the intrapersonal intelligence to grow with God is all about.

14

Praying with Existential Intelligence

*There are times in the lives of all people of conscience
when the truth in one's heart is in such deep opposition
to the falsehood of the world that one must put
everything else in life aside and act upon the truth.*
Sue Frankel-Streit, Catholic worker and peace demonstrator

At one time or another, all of us struggle with the big questions of life: Who am I? Why am I here? What does God want from me? Why does God allow people to suffer? Many of us avoid these questions, but not people with strong existential intelligence. They willingly grapple with such questions, wondering about and seeking the truth.

People with strong existential intelligence revel in asking themselves the hard questions; this is an essential component in the development of their relationship with God.

• One of the best prayers that calls on the existential intelligence is known as "the prayer of the wanted poster." It is relatively easy to pray for the sick, the poor, and those in need. But when we pray for the really "bad" people, as in the prayer of the wanted poster, we are challenged to ask the big questions. Begin this prayer by going to your computer or your post office and making a copy of a wanted poster. Read the description and look at the person as if you were the person's parent. Consider how you would plead for this person before God. Try to come to an understanding of why the person would commit such a crime. Was he or she the victim of poverty? A poor family life? Is he or she guilty? Remind yourself that Jesus was crucified between two criminals. Put the wanted person before God. If you feel anger toward the person, put yourself before God and ask that your heart might open to this person. Keep the poster in a prominent spot and continue to put the person before God.

• Labyrinths first came to be used as a form of prayer in medieval times. Their use has found new popularity in recent years. Many people think of them as mazes, but a labyrinth is different. Walking the labyrinth is a pilgrimage of concentration and focus, a time to consider both the journey and your quest. It is time to ask yourself questions, to reflect, and to draw strength from within. To find a labyrinth near you, go to the Website "Labyrinth Locator." Set a time to go and experience God on the journey with you through this prayer form. Write an account of your time, remembering that we are all called to journey, all called to seek God.

If you can't find a full-sized labyrinth near you, you can make a smaller paper version and follow it with your finger. Find a picture of a labyrinth that appeals to you in a book or on the Web. Then enlarge it to fit on an 8 x 11 sheet of paper. Before you begin your prayer, decide what aspect of your life, what problem, or what inspiration you are seeking to clarify. Start your journey with a prayer asking God to bless this time. As you slowly start your journey by using your finger to "walk" the path of the labyrinth, become aware of what you are feeling. When you reach the center, pause for quiet reflection. Spend time at the center offering thanks and praise. Return to the beginning of the labyrinth, tracing your route carefully. Remind yourself that all beginnings are endings, and vice versa. Close your prayer time by writing or drawing or noting in some way the interior discoveries you have made.

• The Salesian devotions were developed by St. Francis de Sales, who lived in the 1500s. This way of prayer appeals to those who ask:: What do I really believe? To pray in the Salesian way, begin by choosing a concept or topic, for example, one of the mysteries of faith. Francis suggests four ways of coming into God's presence: 1) recognizing that God is everywhere, 2) remembering that God is present in your heart, 3) knowing that God is watching as you pray, and 4) believing that God is actually present with you. Next, focus on the subject you have chosen. Select one or two points of the subject and take time to reflect on their meaning. Savor these points but don't exhaust them. Relish the feelings of love toward God that arise, and be open to any suggestions from God to apply to your life. Close your prayer time by thanking God for what you have learned, and ask for God's help as you use what you have learned to grow in your faith.

• Practicing "emptiness" is another good way to use existential intelligence. Emptiness is a part of life. We need it in order to grow, much like the farmer needs to let the land lay fallow for a time if he wants the seeds to grow well. To begin, take time to become still, being aware of God's presence. Let your body relax; let go of your thoughts as much as possible. Focus on your stillness, and feel the emptiness inside. Remain this way for a while, then begin to see God there holding you, breathing life through you, filling you with love.

• To allow the intrapersonal and existential intelligences to grow in us and in our prayer, it is essential that silence be part of our prayer encounters. To practice, have a meal in silence, or silently do a task you normally would do with music or the television on in the background. God speaks to us in silence. Just as a married couple can be contently in the same room together without saying anthing, so we can be content with God. In silence we reach a moment when it is enough just to be with God and share feelings of warmth and tenderness.

• The Suplician approach to prayer originated with Cardinal de Berulle and Father Jean Jacques Olier, who founded the Society of St. Suplice in Paris in 1641. This approach allows those with strong existential intelligence an opportunity to reflect on the virtues necessary for growth.

Preparation for Suplician prayer begins the night before. Select a virtue to focus on, perhaps one of Jesus' virtues. You might also look through Scripture for passages that speak of this virtue. Keep the virtue in mind as you go to sleep. When you wake up the next morning, begin your meditation. Remember that God is with you. Ask guidance as you consider the virtue. Think about the virtue as shown by Jesus. Now reflect on how well you do or do not live this virtue in your own life. Open your heart to growing in the virtue, and consider specific ways to nurture it. Draw your time to a close by thanking God for bestowing blessings on you, and ask help to grow in this virtue.

When you use your existential intelligence in your prayer encounters with God, you ask the big questions and think about what it is you believe. You explore everything. As you talk with God, you find out more about yourself and the world, enabling you to grow in faith, hope, and love.

15

Multiple Intelligences & Community

We have stories to tell, stories that provide wisdom about the journey of life. What more have we to give one another than our "truth" about our human adventure as honestly and as openly as we know how.

Rabbi Saul Rubin

During her junior year of college, my daughter, Petra, went to the University of Cape Town in South Africa. While there, she had the privilege and challenge of working in a township of women and children who were either HIV-positive or had full-blown cases of AIDS. She grew to know the women as she taught lessons on nutrition, went on picnics with them, and listened to their stories.

Petra grew very close to some of the women, and she found it difficult to leave when her time there was completed. She felt a connectedness to these people and to their families that did not end with her return home.

Later, I found a saying from the Xhosa tribe of Africa that explained Petra's feelings, her care and concern about these people that extended beyond her daily contact with them. The saying reads, "I am because we are." In other words, we are all connected: what happens to one of us happens to us all. Without that realization, our relationship with God cannot blossom. We are family through all that happens, and we are family in prayer. "I am because we are."

Yet although we are God's family, we often don't know how to pray together. When we do, we seldom make use of multiple intelligences. Multiple intelligences flow through community prayer, however, often without our knowing it.

In northern Minnesota the small towns each have their own parish churches in which, because of the small-town influence, the emphasis is on community. This is best evidenced in what happens when someone dies. First, people from the parish arrive at the home shortly after the death to help in whatever way they can. Meanwhile, other people at the church begin a telephone tree to get the word out, and to line up meals for the family and food for the funeral meal.

The funeral choir is called and songs are carefully chosen. On the day of the funeral, the church is generally full, regardless of whether the person was well-known or unknown. After the burial, everyone gathers in the church basement to talk, share food, and remember the deceased.

Multiple intelligences are flowing throughout this event. Bodily-kinesthetic intelligence is being used to clean the family's house or prepare the meals. Those using interpersonal intelligence are making the phone calls, and the naturalist intelligence is helping to prepare the body for burial. The logical-mathematical intelligence is being used to plan the funeral, while the musical-rhythmic is guiding the choice of songs. The visual-spatial people are arranging the flowers. Verbal-linguistic intelligence helps in the writing of the homily, and the intrapersonal and existential intelligences are present in the talk of life everlasting and resurrection.

How well we see the intelligences operating through this community event! Our lives as a community would be richer if we were more aware of how to use multiple intelligences throughout our parish, community, and family life.

Earlier in this book I mentioned the ritual of the Paschal Meal which we hold every year on Holy Thursday. It has become for our family and friends an expression of our community. Different people gather at each celebration, yet there are always some seated at the table who have been there year after year. We sit together at a long table. We all drink from the one bowl of wine and share one matzo. We tell stories of each other's families and recall memories of past meals. We laugh together, we cry together, and we talk about politics, religion, and family. During that evening, we are very much in tune with what it means to be God's family.

All of us belong to God's family. We are called to live with other people. On a small scale, this means the family unit. On a larger scale, it is the town we live in, the friends we make, and the place we work. On an even larger scale, it is our connection with the people of Cambodia, the people of the Sudan, all people across the world. We are connected with the newborn baby in Iceland and the dying soldier in Iraq. We are bound together with dictators and holy people. We are all brothers and sisters.

When we pray together, we bring all those family members with us. We put them before God. We love them before God. By bringing them before God, we let God know that we care, that we love, that we want what is best for everyone. Praying in this way admonishes us to treat one another more attentively.

I once received a card from a friend that showed the silhouette of children running, trying to get a kite into the air. Big, billowy clouds raced across the background. When I opened the card, it read, "I will not raise my child to kill your child." When we talk about community prayer, we talk about embracing each person in love. This means that we realize that we do not kill members of our family, that we seek instead answers to help work things out without violence.

We Are All Connected

• Praying the news is an excellent community prayer encounter, encompassing all the intelligences. To use this approach, have everyone who will be praying together watch the evening news or read the newspaper. Read or listen to the stories carefully. Become aware of the victims, of the perpetrators. List them if you are so inclined. Draw sketches if that is your strength. When the news draws to a close or you turn the last page of the paper, set everything aside. When you have an opportunity to pray together, all of you should bring your notes or sketches. Become aware of God among you, listening, loving. Next, share some of the stories. Talk about the victims and the perpetrators. Share the feelings each of you had as you heard or read the stories.

It is important that this type of prayer does not become a time for people to complain about the government, a particular country, or a group of people. When this happens, stop. Remember you are all family, and you are all responsible for the actions that take place.

Now consider what you are doing, individually and

together, for the people in the news stories. As a group, consider: Where do we stand on some of these issues? Most importantly, how do we behave toward those who are hurting? This particular point in the prayer can be overwhelming. How can we possibly make a difference? This is where we ask God for help, and where we put the people—victims and perpetrators alike—before God. Together as family, love them and ask God to help them, giving them the strength, courage, and change of heart they need.

When this crucial part of the prayer draws to a close, move as a group toward thanksgiving. Thank God for those people who are working on the front lines to eliminate prejudice. Thank God for those who help people in need. Thank God for giving these people the grace to do what they do. Whatever comes to mind from a grateful heart, give voice to it with words, music, or dance. Close your time together with quiet reflection on the mystery of God in our lives. Become aware of how God continues to work in human history. As each of you head home, leave each other with a hug, an expression of your love for one another.

Indeed, we are all brothers and sisters and when we pray with others, we are bringing all those family members with us. In prayer, we put them before God, who knows and loves us all deeply. In the act of bringing them before God, we let God know that we too care, we too love, we too want what is best for them.

A prayer experience like the one above calls us to change and grow. Perhaps it also calls us to shop more carefully, to be more aware of what we really need and what is just a desire. Or it might inspire us to cook a meal using a menu from a different country so that we can experience what the people there have for nourishment each day. Maybe it will inspire us to write our congressional representatives and ask that they take positive action on a particular issue. Whatever it is, we act on the conviction that we are all God's people, and we are all connected.

The Intelligences in Group Prayer

All the intelligences are present in group prayer because each individual brings his or her own strengths and talents to the prayer time. It is only when these strengths and talents are overlooked by other members of the group, or when the group settles on a "one way to pray" approach, that difficulties arise. To avoid this, consider the following for group prayer times:

Use each of the intelligences in this prayer time. Remember that the characteristics of certain intelligences overlap, so something that is geared toward the verbal-linguistic intelligence may also engage the visual-spatial.

Include time for reflection, time for dialogue, and time for thanksgiving. Be sure to allow adequate time for each individual to become aware of God's presence in the group.

Include time for each individual or the group to come up with a resolution to be put into action in the coming weeks. This does not have to be an activity, but it should be something that allows for continued reflection.

Include elements that engage the entire body. This might be something as simple as a handshake or hug or as involved as people moving around the room from object to object. However we do it, it is important that we involve the total body in our group prayer experiences.

Group prayer times should include all peoples. throughout the entire world. Doing so reinforces the understanding that we must continue to grow as a family of God.

• Gathering for an early Christian worship service is a good way to cover all of these points. I don't know who originally put this together—outside of the early Christians, that is!—but I first experienced it in northern Minnesota. People gather together in a room that is dark except for candlelight. There are only a few benches, and many of those in attendance must sit on the floor. This is as it was in the early days of the church, when the Christians were meeting in secret. The benches were for the sick and elderly. The rest of the congregation sat on the floor, stood, or knelt.

The service would open with singing and lots of it! Perhaps people danced in response or even leapt into the air! For a contemporary worship service, invite those in attendance to suggest songs and then begin the singing.

After the singing draws to a natural close, the leader introduces the sharing of Scripture. Again, in the early church, there was no Bible to read from, so the Christians had to share what Scripture they knew by heart. For your worship service, have those gathered share Scripture passages or stories they know well. Welcome them to share even part of a passage; and perhaps someone else in the group can finish it.

Next apply the Scripture to individual lives and to the community. Today this is done in the homily, but in this gathering, have the whole congregation participate. Invite people to talk freely about how they might live this Scripture and thus gain deeper insight into the truths of their faith. Encourage those present to share their own stories, relating how they have grown in their faith and ways that God has been present to them.

After the sharing, it is time for the community prayer. The names of those who are sick or who have died, those who are dealing with problems, and also those who are experiencing good times, are put before God. Finally, the worship service draws to an end with the sharing of bread and wine. In the New Testament, we have evidence of many different communion services. Although this particular one is not Eucharist with a capital "E," it does symbolize our connectedness as a faith family and community.

After the bread and wine are shared, invite participants to say aloud the name of someone who was not able to be present and to take this person a piece of the bread as a reminder that they too belong to the Body of Christ. (This practice was a regular part of the early Church services as well.) A final song brings the worship service to a close.

Although we don't know exactly what took place during those early days of the Church, a service like this helps us to feel connected with the Christians who have gone before us. It lends deeper meaning to the words prayed at Mass: "From age to age you gather a people unto yourself."

Growing Dandelions

Dandelion seeds provide a good image of group prayer. The silvery puff balls that we all try to keep out of our lawns are really a symbol of life. If you look carefully at a dandelion that has gone to seed, you will see that each seed touches six others. By the same token, each seed is strong and independent and capable of becoming a new dandelion. When we gather with a group of believers, we come as individuals, but through our shared prayer, we touch one another at the deepest level. Just as the seeds of the dandelion are all attached to the stem, so we are connected to God and rooted in Jesus.

If we approach prayer with the dandelion in mind, we will

be sensitive to including the multiple intelligences in all of our prayer experiences. We will want the best for both individuals and for the group. We will celebrate our differences as well as our unity, always with the intention of growing together toward God.

16

You as a Gift of God

How can you define prayer except by saying that it is love?
It is love expressed in speech and love expressed in silence.
To put it another way, prayer is the meeting of two loves:
the love of God and our love.

Catherine de Hueck Doherty, justice pioneer

The Danish philosopher Søren Kierkegaard wrote, "Prayer does not change God, but changes the one who prays." When we speak about prayer, we speak about a love relationship between God and us. Because it is a relationship, we have to realize it will change us, as does any relationship in our lives. We will never be the same when we decide to be friends and lovers with God.

Prayer takes many different forms. Through the ages, various people have shown us many ways to enter into a relationship with God. There are the Spiritual Exercises of St. Ignatius, as well as the Franciscan, the Teresian, and the Salesian ways of prayer. There is the prayer of St. Francis of Assisi, the prayer of St. John of the Cross, and the Little Way of St. Thérèse of

Lisieux. There are prayer forms that address temperament and personality and ones that rely on silence and contemplation.

All of these prayer forms are good. We can take something from each of them, but the fact remains that we must pray as we are. We can pray someone else's prayer, but ultimately, God wants *us*. God made each of us unique, and each of us must enter the love relationship with God just as uniquely.

Some people don't have to say much in a relationship: their actions say everything. Some people have to talk with the one they love and stay in touch—with flowers or letters or phone calls. Others have to do things with their beloved—have dinner, play a game, or go off on a weekend of relaxation. So it is in our relationship with God. If we approach it as unique individuals, everything is okay. If we choose to, we don't have to say much. Or we might simply want to cry or laugh or be with God. Maybe we write God a letter or write in our journal about something that we want God to know.

Throughout the ages, saints have shown us that God can be approached in many ways. There have been saints who spent years living and praying alone in caves and others who made pilgrimages to bring them closer to God. There have been those like St. Thérèse, who had such a comfortable relationship with God that she died feeling confident God that would allow her to spend her heaven doing good upon earth. The saints have also shown us there we can take many postures for prayer. Some have lain prostrate during their prayer time; others have stood for long hours with hands outstretched. Some saints sat down, others knelt, and still others danced.

Your might say praying is as different as the marriages around us. No two husbands and wives approach their marriage in the same way. They have their own personalities and their own ways of behaving and communicating, and they enter into the relationship with those individual styles. So too with prayer. We need to be flexible in the ways that we communicate with God. We need to become aware of who we are and where we are in our lives. In this respect, the multiple intelligences can help us to know who we are, find prayer styles that accommodate this, and challenge us to move beyond the comfortable.

"Make Way for the Image of God!"

In the Jewish tradition, there is a story that speaks of the wonderful gift each person is. It says that every time a person walks down the street he or she is preceded by hosts of angels who are saying, "Make way! Make way for the image of God!"

We often skim over the passage in Genesis that tells us man and woman were made in the image and likeness of God. If we were able, even in a small part, to comprehend what this means, nothing in our life would ever be the same. As Thomas Merton wrote:

It is a glorious destiny to be a member of the human race. Now I realize what we are. And if only everybody could realize this! But it cannot be explained. There is no way of telling people that they are all walking around shining like the sun.

Using the multiple intelligences to pray can help us understand that we are indeed children of God, made in God's image. By using our bodies, our spirits, and our minds; by using math, words, and visual images, we move closer to an appreciation of the great gift that we are.

This past August, I was driving with my daughter on the annual trip back to college. As she was now a senior, I knew it would be the last such trip we would take together, a car ride of over a thousand miles. I've always loved these long car rides, because they give us the opportunity to talk without interruption about many different things. This trip was no different. We covered subject after subject, and as the sun began to set, our conversation turned toward religion.

"I have trouble," Petra said, "with putting God 'out there.' I can't. I just feel God here, with me." She pointed to herself. "I can't separate."

Petra is in her early twenties. She still has a sense of wonder, and she uses all of her intelligences well. Granted, she has a lot of life to live, and a lot of things to experience. Undoubtedly, she will have her own faith crisis when she has to consider what it is she really believes. She will struggle with all the big questions. But I am confident of one thing: she will never lose sight of her God because she has discovered the secret that all of us need to discover: God is not "out there"; God is not in church; God is in us.

As you explore using multiple intelligences in your prayer encounters, remember that God wants all of you. Once you begin to experience prayer in its many forms, you'll start to discover all of God's surprises. But the biggest surprise is this: God is hidden right in your heart!

Appendix

Finding Your Strongest Intelligence and Your Way of Prayer

Throughout this book I have talked about the importance of getting in touch with your strongest intelligence, beginning to pray with that intelligence, and then stretching to develop the other intelligences. The following gives an overview of each intelligence along with ways to develop it in your prayer. For further elaboration on the prayer suggestions, please see the chapter corresponding to the intelligence.

Our Creator calls us to develop all of our intelligences. We need to stretch. A friend once told me, "You have to take chances if you really want to live." What better person to take a chance with than God!

Verbal-Linguistic Intelligence

This is the intelligence of words. People strong in this intelligence have a high sensitivity to the different functions of language. They do well using pictures, humor, storytelling, and writing in their prayer.

Ways to Pray with Verbal-Linguistic Intelligence
- Using books for reading and reflection
- Saying familiar prayers with various emotions
- Using mantras
- Writing parables
- Sharing prayer collections
- Praying with the movies
- Praying in tongues

Logical-Mathematical Intelligence

This intelligence loves numerical patterns and long chains of reasoning and is able to see relationships. People with this intelligence thrive on connections and consequences.

Ways to Pray with Logical-Mathematical Intelligence
•Prayers of connection
•Family photo prayer
•Reflections on the lives of the saints
•Internet prayer
•Examination of conscience
•Baking and cooking prayer reflections

Musical-Rhythmic Intelligence

This intelligence produces and appreciates rhythm, pitch, and timbre. It deeply appreciates the various forms of musical expression and is sensitive to the sounds of the environment and the human voice.

Ways To Pray with Musical-Rhythmic Intellence
•Commercials as prayer
•Found sound prayer
•Favorite music prayer reflection
•Singing the blues
•Writing or painting a song
•Drumming
•Awareness of the rhythms of life prayer

Visual-Spatial Intelligence

People with this intelligence can perceive the visual world accurately and then recreate their experience. They see form, color, shape, and texture in their mind's eye and are easily able to transfer those elements to concrete representations.

Ways to Pray with Visual-Spatial Intelligence
•Creation of symbols
•Icon prayer
•Stations of the Cross
•Transformation prayer
•Sacred space use
•Visual boxes

Bodily-Kinesthetic Intelligence

Tastes, smells, and sounds are very much a part of the bodily-kinesthetic intelligence. People strong in this intelligence are sensitive to the movements of their bodies and often use the total body for expression.

Ways to Pray with Bodily-Kinesthetic Intelligence
•Dance and movement prayer
•The Hug Prayer
•Finger prayers
•Making bread prayer
•Clapping prayers
•Walking

Naturalist Intelligence

This intelligence has a sensitivity to the natural world. People graced with it have a keen ability to recognize and categorize plants, animals, and other objects in nature. They appreciate the interaction with creation.

Ways to Pray with Naturalist Intelligence
•Creating a ritual

•Steps-to-growth prayer

•Cloud reflection

•Creation meditation

•Pilgrimage

•Nature sketching

•Gardening

Interpersonal Intelligence

This intelligence has the ability to detect and respond appropriately to the moods, motivations, and desires of others. In harmony with other people, those with this intelligence have the ability to work cooperatively in a group and to communicate both verbally and non-verbally with others.

Ways To Pray with Interpersonal Intelligence
•Prayer of connections

•Celebration of important events

•The blessing cup

•The empty chair

•Loving-kindness prayer

•Making Scripture personal

•Newspaper prayer

Intrapersonal Intelligence

Intrapersonal intelligence people know themselves. They know their feelings and emotional responses and are given to self-reflection. They have a great sense of the spiritual and struggle for insight, always looking for the deeper picture.

Ways to Pray with Intrapersonal Intelligence
•Taking an identity from Scripture
•Sunday comics prayer
•Prayer blanket
•Guided imagery
•Prayer of one word
•Practice of mindfulness
•Dream journal

Existential Intelligence

This intelligence has people asking themselves the hard questions. They look to the total picture of life here and beyond and its implications not only for themselves but for all humankind.

Ways to Pray with Existential Intelligence
•The Wanted Poster prayer
•Labyrinths
•Salesian devotions
•Practice of emptiness
•Prayer of silence
•Sulpician approach

Resources

•*Active Learning Handbook for the Multiple Intelligences Classroom*, James Bellanca, Skylight Books, Arlington Heights, IL, 1997.

•*Anyone Can Pray*, Graeme J. Davidson, Paulist Press, Mahwah, NJ, 1983.

•*Developing Students' Multiple Intelligences*, Kristen Nicholson-Nelson, Professional Books, New York, NY, 1998.

•*Frames of Mind*, Howard Gardner, Basic Books, New York, NY, 1983, 2004.

•*Finding God in the Dark: Taking the Spiritual Exercises of St. Ignatius to the Movies*, John Pungente, SJ, and Monty Williams, SJ, Pauline Publishing, Boston, MA, 2005.

•*Intelligence Reframed: Multiple Intelligences for the 21st Century*, Howard Gardner, Basic Books, New York, NY, 1999.

•*Meditation: The Complete Guide*, Patricia Monaghan & Eleanor G. Biereck, New World Library, Novato, CA, 1999.

•*Multiple Intelligences: The Theory in Practice*, Howard Gardner, Basic Books, New York, NY, 1993.

•*Praying Always: A Multiple Intelligences Approach to Prayer*, Caroljean Willie, Harcourt Religion Publishers, Orlando, FL, 2003.

•*Sacred Rituals*, Eileen London and Belinda Recio, Fair Winds Publishers, Gloucester, MA, 2004.

•*Spiritual Literacy: Reading the Sacred in Everyday life*, Frederic and Mary Ann Brussat, Scribner, New York, NY, 1996.

•*Spiritual RX*, Frederic and Mary Ann Brussat, Hyperion, New York, NY, 2000.

•*7 Kinds of Smart: Identifying and Developing Your Many Intelligences*, Thomas Armstrong, Plume Books, New York, NY, 1993.